7

Aspects of modern sociology

The social structure of modern Britain

GENERAL EDITORS

John Barron Mays
Eleanor Rathbone Professor of Social Science, University of Liverpool

Maurice Craft
Senior Lecturer in Education, University of Exeter

Wage Regulation under the Statute of Artificers (*1938*)
Applications for Admission to Universities (*1957*)
Women and Teaching (*1963*)
Higher Civil Servants in Britain (*2nd impression 1966*)
Six Years After (*with A. Poole and A. Kuhn*, 1970*)

Population

R. K. Kelsall M.A.

Professor and Head of Department of Sociological Studies
University of Sheffield

Longman

LONGMAN GROUP LIMITED
London

Associated companies, branches and representatives throughout the world

© *R. K. Kelsall 1967, 1970, 1972*
First published 1967
Revised 1970
Second edition 1972

ISBN 0 582 48709 9 (Paper)

Printed in Great Britain by
Lowe & Brydone (Printers) Ltd.,
London

326 374

Contents

Editors' Preface   vii
Foreword   ix

  1 Sources of misunderstanding   1
  2 Types of population data   5
  3 The trend of Britain's population to 1961   14
  4 Fertility   18
  5 Mortality   24
  6 Immigration and emigration   29
  7 Internal migration   38
  8 Social class variations in mortality and fertility   47
  9 Other social implications of demographic data   58
 10 Forecasting the future: the population at large   69
 11 Forecasting the future: manpower, general and skilled   80
 12 Theories and policies   87
References and further reading   95
Appendix 1: Standard Regions of England and Wales   103
Map: Density of population 1961   106
Map: Percentage change in population 1951–61   107
Appendix 2: Some very recent developments   108
Index   123

Editors' Preface

British higher education is now witnessing a very rapid expansion of teaching and research in the social sciences, and, in particular, in sociology. This new series has been designed for courses offered by universities, colleges of education, colleges of technology, and colleges of further education to meet the needs of students training for social work, teaching and a wide variety of other professions. It does not attempt a comprehensive treatment of the whole field of sociology, but concentrates on the social structure of modern Britain which forms a central feature of most university and college sociology courses in this country. Its purpose is to offer an analysis of our contemporary society through the study of basic demographic, ideological and structural features, and through the study of such major social institutions as the family, education, the economic and political structure, and so on.

The aim has been to produce a series of introductory texts which will in combination form the basis for a sustained course of study, but each volume has been designed as a single whole and can be read in its own right.

We hope that the topics covered in the series will prove attractive to a wide reading public and that, in addition to students, others who wish to know more than is readily available about the nature and structure of their own society will find them of interest.

JOHN BARRON MAYS
MAURICE CRAFT

Foreword

The dearth of up-to-date, introductory accounts of Britain's present and expected future population position amounts almost to a famine. Had this not been so, I would never have accepted the invitation of the editors of the present series to try and fill this gap. However, the appearance of the present book will, it is to be hoped, have two consequences. First, more people will be led to take an interest in our current mortality, fertility and migration trends and their possible implications, and to follow up some of the lines of enquiry indicated here. Secondly, some of those to whose specialised work reference has been made throughout this book may be encouraged, or goaded, into making a better job of introducing the reader to this fascinating field than I have managed to do. In either case the enterprise will have been well worth while.

R. K. KELSALL

With demographic as with any other type of data there are conventional usages and other possible sources of error or misunderstanding of which it is desirable to be aware before attempting to make use of published figures. Though attention will be drawn to these as occasion arises in the chapters that follow, it seemed worth while to discuss a few of the more important ones at the very outset.

Varying meanings of the term 'population'

It is natural to assume that 'the population of a particular area at a particular date' can mean only one thing, but there are in Britain a variety of different 'populations' to which such a description could apply. The *enumerated* population is, of course, the number who, on the occasion of an actual count (e.g. a population census) were found to be in a given area, whether this was in some cases accidental or not. The *resident* population excludes those enumerated in an area who are not normally resident there, and includes those who, though not in the area when the count was taken, normally reside there. The *home* or *de facto* population of, for example, England and Wales, is the number of people of all types believed actually to be there. The *total* population is the home population *plus* members of H.M. Forces belonging to England and Wales but serving overseas, *minus* the Forces of other countries temporarily in England and Wales. The *civilian* population is the total population *minus* members of H.M. Forces belonging to England and Wales wherever they are. The use of the adjectives *projected* and *estimated* requires no special explanation. Care has clearly to be exercised in comparing population figures to ensure that the same type of population is involved. For some purposes one type may be more appropriate than another. It goes without saying that the population of an area at different dates should not be compared unless the appropriate adjustment has been made for any boundary changes that may have taken place.

Separate figures for the sexes

Wherever the experience of one sex is markedly different from that of the other, it is important to have separate figures. This is, for example, true in most countries of life expectancy; a figure of expectation of life at birth combining the two sexes is, therefore, much less useful than figures for each sex separately.

Separate figures for different age groups

The same argument holds good here. The mortality experience of the varying age groups tends to differ, and if a single figure for all ages is required, it should (as with standard mortality ratios) take into account the varying proportions both of people and of deaths in each of the different age groups.

The 'population at risk'

Putting some of these matters in more general form, if a rate per thousand is being given, it is important that the thousand should be as close as possible to the 'population at risk'. To take a simple example, to express a birth rate as the number of births in a given period per thousand population would be crude, and of little value; to refine it by confining the population figure to women would be better; to refine it still further by relating the number of births to the number of women of child-bearing age would be better still. A more sophisticated example may show both how important and how difficult it often is to find a reasonable approximation to the population at risk. Suppose that we want to show the changing propensity of school-leavers of middle-class as against working-class origin to embark on a course of teacher-training. The figure of entrants to such training at the usual ages can be broken down into its sex and social class components, but what is the appropriate population at risk? Merely to take the whole population of young men and women of the appropriate age in these social class groups would be misleading, since we know that many of them would not have the educational qualifications to be eligible for teacher training whether they wanted to embark on such a training or not. So we would have to reduce the population at risk either to those possessing evidence of having attained the minimum level and type of education required; or, if the data needed to make such an estimate were lacking, to take the nearest approximation to it, such as the population of young men and women of working-class and middle-class origin respectively who had remained at school beyond a certain age. Only then could we hope, by comparing prewar with postwar data, to show in a meaningful way the changing propensity of young people with different family backgrounds to embark on teacher-training rather than on some other form of training or employment.

Varying completeness and accuracy of basic data

There are two main types of possibility here. First, there is the failure of certain cases to be recorded or enumerated at all, so that the figures are an understatement of the true position. Secondly, the information recorded about a case may be incorrect, either owing to negligence on the part of the official or of the person supplying the information. To give only one example, it has long been realised that, when registering a death, relatives may feel no harm is done by upgrading the occupation of the person who has died; this so-called 'halo-effect' may to an unknown extent distort any picture based on taking such occupational data as completely reliable.

Sampling instead of a complete count

There is an increasing tendency to elicit information from a sample rather than from the whole population. This procedure is cheaper, puts the population at large to much less trouble, and often enables results to be published more quickly. It does have the disadvantage, however, that anyone 'grossing up' the published figures has to exercise appropriate caution in their use, and should have made himself aware of the limitations to which they are subject. In all the census volumes based on answers from a 10 per cent sample of the population there is, for example, a comprehensive introductory statement of the limitations that apply to the data presented.

Types of population data

The range and complexity of data collected at the time of a population census can be illustrated by running through the main types of question asked at the England and Wales 1961 Census. First, the basic facts of sex, age, marital condition and relationship to the head of the household were sought, much as they had been on previous occasions. Questions on usual residence, on birthplace and nationality, on occupation, industry and place of work were again included, though not always in exactly the same form as previously. The question on the age at which full-time education ceased, first asked in 1951, was extended to the population generally. Another group of 1951 questions, on whether the household had sole or shared use of a cold water tap, a hot water tap, a fixed bath, a water closet, was repeated. And for those in Wales and Monmouthshire, a question on ability to speak Welsh (first asked in 1891) was also included.

Some entirely new types of question (as distinct from elaboration of questions formerly asked) were added in 1961. Information was sought, for example, on whether householders were owner-occupiers, Council tenants, or tenants of other kinds. If someone was not gainfully employed, an indication was asked for as to which of a number of possible reasons for this state of affairs applied in this case. If gainful employment was part-time, the number of hours worked was sought. The possession of certain scientific and technological qualifications was recorded. There were also new questions to throw light on the frequency, amount, duration and characteristics of population movements within the country, and the degree of permanence of one's usual residence.

Taking questions of a type asked at previous censuses and those introduced for the first time in 1961 together, the list is clearly a formidable one. On this particular occasion it was decided not to ask everyone the full range of questions, but to restrict this burden to a 10 per cent sample of households (and of those living in institutions and hotels). This new procedure had several results. First, it meant that nine out of ten people were, in 1961, actually asked for less information than at any previous census this century. Secondly, it meant that where data only collected from the 10 per cent sample were involved, the tables of figures published had to relate to that sample, and were subject to the limitations imposed by the sampling procedure. This did not merely apply to the questions asked for the first time in 1961, but also to many types of question to which answers had previously been sought for the whole relevant population. The questions chosen for sample treatment were those relating to occupation, employment, place of work, status in employment, education, scientific and technological qualifications, change of usual residence or duration of stay at present usual address, and persons usually resident in private households who were absent on Census night. Of the separate volumes of tables so far published giving data of various types on a national basis or for large areas, therefore, the main ones including the *whole* relevant population are the age, marital condition and general tables, and those relating to buildings, dwellings and households, usual residence, birthplace and nationality. Those on a 10 per cent sample basis include those relating to occupation, socio-economic group, workplace, industry, migration and duration of residence, Commonwealth immigrants in the conurbations, education and the possession of certain scientific and technological qualifications. The volume of fertility tables includes some relating to the whole relevant population and some based on the 10 per cent sample: it is worth noting that the questions bearing on fertility were fuller than at any previous *census*, but in some respects fell short of what had been elicited at the voluntary Family Census of 1946.

Comparability between figures relating to different census dates is often, as we know, impaired by changes in classification. We are, for example, warned that 'comparison of occupation figures for 1951 and 1961 is very difficult, as the occupation classification has been completely revised'. Revision of the allocation of occupations to the five social classes and the fifteen socio-economic groups nearly always takes place at the time of a census, so that this type of material is doubly dangerous for purposes of comparison over time. It is worth noting, incidentally, that the main framework of the *industrial* classification remained the same in 1961 as it had been in 1951.

The idea of only putting the heads of one in ten of the households of the country to the trouble of providing some of the required information was evidently felt to have been a good one, both from the public relations and from the national expenditure point of view. For when it was decided to have a further population census after only five years, on 24 April 1966, it was also decided to confine the *entire* enquiry to a 10 per cent sample. It seems highly probable that, in future, we shall have such a census at five-yearly instead of ten-yearly intervals; and that censuses will in future be based either wholly or partly on a sample instead of on all households. The questions asked in the 1966 census kept broadly to the 1961 pattern, but amongst the new or extended types of information sought, several are important enough to be mentioned. These included certain data on car ownership and garaging, and on means of transport to and from one's place of work; usual address not merely a year ago (as in 1961) but also five years ago; and being asked to list any educational qualifications obtained since reaching the age of 18. The first tables resulting from the 1966 Census are not expected to appear until the Spring of 1967.

An interesting example both of the possibilities and the limitations of a population census as a means of obtaining usable data of a rather different kind to that hitherto obtained is provided by the case of the 1961 attempt to find out facts about the number and occupational distribution of people possessing certain scientific and technological qualifications. The main reason for including this question was that the Minister for Science had requested that data of this kind should be collected to supplement the inadequate information previously available to committees concerned with scientific manpower estimation and related problems. Previous enquiries into the number and distribution of scientists had been conducted by the Ministry of Labour in 1956 and 1959 (and others were undertaken in 1962 and 1965), but they were subject to several obvious limitations. First, they were *voluntary* enquiries. Secondly, the fact of the approach being to the *employer* rather than to the qualified person himself was clearly far from satisfactory, and could produce misleading results. Thirdly, only a sample of employers engaged in a limited range of industrial activity was approached, so that many qualified persons working in other fields were not represented in the sample at all.

The question on this subject in the 1961 Census was restricted to the 10 per cent sample. The information was asked for in respect of *all* persons in that sample, irrespective of their current occupation, who held one or more of a list of qualifications in a branch of science or technology (excluding medicine, dentistry, pharmacy, optics, veterinary science, architecture, economics, geography and the social sciences). The list included University degrees and diplomas, qualifications of equal standard awarded by other educational institutions, and corporate membership of certain professional institutions. Some 28,761 people on the census schedules for England and Wales and for Scotland were found to possess one or more of these qualifications. In view of the smallness of the number of cases in the sample and for other reasons, it was decided to publish the figures on a Great Britain basis only, and not for the countries separately. In what follows, the sample figures are 'grossed up' by adding a zero to the actual number in the sample.

Taking all those found to possess one or more of the qualifications, their sex and age distribution is shown in Table 1. It can be seen that, in the case of males, the younger the age group the higher the proportion possessing these qualifications, showing that the increasing demand for men with a scientific or engineering training has produced an increasing supply of them. In the case of females, only the youngest and oldest age groups show the influence of increasing demand. Some of the people concerned were 'economically inactive'. The main categories involved here were the retired (17,510), postgraduate students (9,870), and others (10,370); the great majority of the latter were women, presumably engaged in household duties. Subtracting the economically inactive of all types left an economically active total of 249,800, of whom only 18,300 were women. The number actually in employment at the time of the census was 1,830 less than this. Six industrial groups, with 10,000 or more of these qualified persons each, accounted for three-quarters of the total. Professional and Scientific Services had the lion's share (82,350),

TABLE I

Number and proportion of men and women in Great Britain in 1961 possessing specified scientific and technological qualifications (based on 10 per cent sample)

Sex and Age Group	Estimated 1961 Population	Persons possessing the specified qualifications	
		Number	Percentage
Males:			
Under 25	No relevant figure	21,940	No relevant percentage
25–34	3,262,000	82,830	2·54
35–44	3,438,000	62,140	1·81
45–54	3,493,000	41,210	1·18
55–64	2,777,000	29,800	1·07
65 and over	2,334,000	18,020	0·77
Females:			
Under 25	No relevant figure	4,080	No relevant percentage
25–34	3,220,000	9,550	0·30
35–44	3,517,000	5,670	0·16
45–54	3,634,000	5,330	0·15
55–64	3,222,000	4,740	0·15
65 and over	3,733,000	2,300	0·06

Source. Census 1961, Great Britain: Scientific and Technological Qualifications.
Note. Sample numbers have been 'grossed up'.

followed by Engineering and Electrical Goods (38,310), Chemicals and Allied Industries (19,480), Public Administration and Defence (19,130), Vehicles (13,340) and Gas, Electricity and Water (12,280).

It is also possible to indicate the broad nature of the *occupational* distribution of the whole body of qualified persons who were economically active (including the 1,830 who were not in employment at the time of the census). Of the 18,300 qualified women who were economically active, over 90 per cent were in the group 'Professional, Technical Workers, Artists'; within that group, 72 per cent were engaged in teaching of some kind, and 12 per cent were chemists or physical and biological scientists. Of the 231,500 qualified men who were economically active, three-quarters were in the group 'Professional, Technical Workers, Artists'; within that group civil, structural, municipal, mechanical and electrical engineers and other technologists accounted for 31 per cent, but other important sub-categories included those engaged in teaching of some kind (22 per cent), chemists and physical and biological scientists (17 per cent), and laboratory assistants and technicians and technical workers not elsewhere classified (i.e. those engaged in technical as opposed to technological occupations) who formed 5 per cent of the group total. The only other occupational group with as much as 10 per cent of the economically active qualified men was 'Administrators and Managers' with 15 per cent.

Although it is natural to ask how far this occupational distribution appears to show a waste of qualified manpower, the material is not well suited to providing a useful answer to such a question. For while the recording of qualifications was not, it is true, in any way dependent on their use in the occupation followed, and although particular occupations (such as that of the clergy, with $1,470 \pm 240$ scientists and technologists) can clearly hardly make substantial use of these types of training, who can say how many of the 35,580 men classified as administrators and managers would, from a national point of view, have been making better use of their paper qualifications in some other type of occupation? The official report, apart from drawing attention to a number of possible cases of misuse of skilled manpower (notably the graduate laboratory assistants and laboratory technicians), contents itself with the suitably guarded generalisation: 'it is indeed clear that many persons are employed on work which has no relationship to the scientific or engineering qualifications they possess'.

Mention may be made of one other matter on which information has hitherto been completely lacking, namely the extent to which scientists and technologists living and working in Britain were born overseas. So far as those possessing qualifications of the type under discussion are concerned, the foreign-born proportion turns out to be surprisingly small, only 8 per cent; in nationality terms, only a little over 1 per cent of the qualified were aliens.

Individualised data possibilities

Speaking very generally, we have hitherto had to depend for our picture of the British population on data originating in two ways, by census-type enquiries and by registration. In the first case, of which the population census itself is an obvious example, all or a sample of those possessing a particular characteristic (such as that of residing in a given area) are questioned at what is, for them, an arbitrary point in time; other examples of the same technique include follow-up studies of those who completed a particular form of education or training in a given year. The second type of data, in terms of origin, derives from particular events taking place and being registered, the occasion being taken to ask questions relating to those involved; apart from birth, marriage and death registration, other familiar examples include registration of entry to or completion of courses of study or types of employment. However valuable the material arising in both these ways may be, it suffers from one obvious and grave defect, that the possibilities of linking together data originating in different ways to show the direction and nature of movement over time are strictly limited. They are limited by the circumstance that the individuals to whom the particulars relate lose their identity in the process of assembling and processing the data, so that potential links with data from other sources are destroyed. One has only to think of the labour involved (even if permission to consult the records were given) in piecing together the basic demographic, educational and occupational data for the members of only *one* household from standard census and registration sources, central and local, to realise how impossible it is to form an adequate picture, even in outline, of what is happening, without a proliferation of *ad hoc* enquiries far beyond acceptable limits. Fortunately there is a possible way out of

·this difficulty, and it seems certain that it will increasingly have to be adopted.

The solution is, of course, to provide everyone (ideally at birth, but perhaps initially later) with an identification number which would subsequently form an essential part of all official registration and record-keeping throughout that individual's life. Published figures could still be in anonymous statistical form, but the essential links between data relating to the same person but arising at different times and in different ways would be preserved, so that all the relevant material for any given purpose could be put together at any time without the need for special additional enquiries. As an example of the possibilities opened up by a full-blown policy of data collection on an individualised basis, it could then be shown in statistically reliable form how the first-born fared in educational and occupational terms by comparison with second, third or later children; how only children compared in these respects with those from families of other sizes; how, for any given birth-order or family-size situation, those from different social strata or different regions fared, and so on. Again, instead of having to mount special enquiries to discover what had happened to those of given educational attainment or with particular types of training, their present occupations and areas of residence would emerge as a by-product of routine data collection.

The inevitable objection to what, on the face of it, is an eminently sensible procedure both from the individual's and the community's point of view is, of course, the danger of misuse of the material assembled in this way. The idea that for every citizen there is, in effect, a 'dossier' of basic personal information in official records conjures up horrifying possibilities of such information being used to his or her disadvantage by unscrupulous officials or unscrupulous Governments, and it is easy to suggest that only in wartime could such a potentially dangerous infringement of personal privacy be contemplated. Stringent safeguards would clearly have to be provided, both in terms of the publication and the use of such data. It is worth remembering, however, that a great deal of information about all of us is already collected and stored and made available for approved purposes; the change would be not so much that new types of information would be involved, but that data of roughly the existing type would be capable of assembly and presentation in a much more meaningful (though still statistically anonymous) form. The gain, in terms of being able for the first time to base social policy on adequate factual information about the present and past situation, would be enormous; the loss, in terms of potential dangers to the individual could, with appropriate safeguards, be negligible.

The trend of Britain's population to 1961

3

It is reasonable for the layman to ask the question 'What is the total population of Britain, and how has it changed since the beginning of this century?' Before an answer can be given, however, the various areas which in the aggregate constitute Britain in one or other of its possible meanings have to be considered. The British Isles, comprising England and Wales, Scotland, Northern Ireland, Eire, the Isle of Man, and the Channel Islands, had in 1961 a population of some $55\frac{1}{2}$ million, or about 14 million more than in 1901, an increase of 34 per cent. At the earlier date, England (excluding Monmouthshire) accounted for about 73 per cent of this total, Scotland for some 11 per cent, what is now Eire for 8 per cent or so, Wales and Monmouthshire for less than 5 per cent, what is now Northern Ireland for 3 per cent, and the Isle of Man and the Channel Islands between them for about one-half of 1 per cent. At the later date, England (excluding Monmouthshire) accounted for a higher proportion of the total (78 per cent), Wales and Monmouthshire for about the same proportion as before, and the remaining countries for somewhat less than before (notably Eire, which by 1961 only accounted for 5 per cent of the British Isles total). If by Britain's population we mean the population of the United Kingdom, or Great Britain and Northern Ireland, we have to exclude from the figures Eire, the Isle of Man and the Channel Islands. On this basis the population increase between 1901 and 1961 becomes $14\frac{1}{2}$ million instead of 14 million, a percentage increase of 38 per cent as against 34 per cent for the British Isles as a whole.

The main reason for this difference is that Eire experienced a *decline* in population between these two dates of about 13 per cent. Great Britain on its own has experienced a slightly larger proportionate increase in population than has the United Kingdom (39 per cent instead of 38 per cent); and this in its turn is due to Northern Ireland having had a much smaller increase in population (15 per cent) between these two dates than was experienced by England and Wales. Of the other constituent units of the United Kingdom, Scotland's population increase between these two dates was not unlike that of Northern Ireland and amounted to 16 per cent. England and Wales experienced the largest percentage increase in population, 42 per cent, and Wales and Monmouthshire an intermediate rate of 31 per cent. These differences in rates of population increase amongst the constituent countries of the present United Kingdom are mainly due to the migration factor; they are not the result of any large differences in either fertility or mortality.

Responsibility for the collection and regular publication of population data rests with separate Registrars General for England and Wales, for Scotland and for Northern Ireland. Although *some* figures are regularly published for two or more of these units jointly (i.e. Great Britain, or Great Britain and Northern Ireland), it is often more convenient to discuss data for England and Wales alone. Where only a broad picture is required, and where care is taken to draw attention to any major differences in particular factors between the constituent countries, no great harm need result from using the England and Wales figures as a guide to the position in the country as a whole. England and Wales, it may be noted, accounted for 87 per cent of the population of Great Britain and Northern Ireland in 1961, and 90 per cent of the population of Great Britain.

Carrying the story back to the beginning of the nineteenth century, the population of Great Britain (i.e. England and Wales and Scotland) has risen from some $10\frac{1}{2}$ million in 1801 to about $51\frac{1}{4}$ million in 1961. The rate of growth was much faster in the early part of that period than it has been more recently. Table 2 shows the mean annual rate of change in each intercensal period for England and Wales and for Scotland separately. Until after the 1881 Census, this average annual intercensal rate of growth varied, for England and Wales, from a little under $1\frac{1}{4}$ per cent to a little over $1\frac{3}{4}$ per cent; while in Scotland the rate of growth tended to be somewhat lower,

Intercensal population changes for England and Wales and for Scotland, 1801–1961

TABLE 2

	ENGLAND AND WALES			SCOTLAND		
	Population	Increase or decrease since previous census	Mean annual rate of intercensal increase or decrease	Population	Increase or decrease since previous census	Mean annual rate of intercensal increase or decrease
1801	8,892,536	—	—	1,608,420	—	—
1811	10,164,256	+1,271,720	+1·43	1,805,864	+197,444	+1·23
1821	12,000,236	+1,835,980	+1·81	2,091,521	+285,657	+1·58
1831	13,896,797	+1,896,561	+1·58	2,364,386	+272,865	+1·30
1841	15,914,148	+2,017,351	+1·45	2,620,184	+255,798	+1·08
1851	17,927,609	+2,013,461	+1·26	2,888,742	+268,558	+1·02
1861	20,066,224	+2,138,615	+1·19	3,062,294	+173,552	+0·60
1871	22,712,266	+2,646,042	+1·32	3,360,018	+297,724	+0·97
1881	25,974,439	+3,262,173	+1·44	3,735,573	+375,555	+1·12
1891	29,002,525	+3,028,086	+1·17	4,025,647	+290,074	+0·78
1901	32,527,843	+3,525,318	+1·22	4,472,103	+446,456	+1·11
1911	36,070,492	+3,542,649	+1·09	4,760,904	+288,801	+0·65
1921	37,886,699	+1,816,207	+0·50	4,882,497	+121,593	+0·26
1931	39,952,377	+2,065,678	+0·55	4,842,980	− 39,517	−0·08
1951	43,757,888	+2,297,888	+0·29	5,096,415	+253,435	+0·26
1961	46,104,548	+2,346,660	+0·54	5,178,490	+ 82,075	+0·16

Source. Census Reports of Registrars General for England and Wales and Scotland.
Note. The mean annual rates of intercensal increase or decrease are simply one-tenth (or, in the case of 1931–51, one-twentieth) of the percentage change over the intercensal period; they are not weighted or adjusted in any way, and therefore differ in some respects from those published in the General Report on the England and Wales 1961 Census.

varying from just over one-half of 1 per cent to $1\frac{1}{2}$ per cent. From then until the 1911 Census the England and Wales rate of increase fluctuated between 1 per cent and $1\frac{1}{4}$ per cent, and the Scottish one averaged less than 1 per cent. The 1921 Census, coming as it did after a major world war involving a very heavy death roll, was bound to show a much lower mean annual rate of increase since the previous census than had hitherto been recorded; the England and Wales rate fell to one-half of 1 per cent, and the Scottish rate was as low as one-quarter of 1 per cent. From then until the 1961 Census (and spreading the 1931–51 change over twenty years instead of ten) the rate of growth in England and Wales has never approached the pre-1911 level, but has fluctuated between roughly one-quarter of 1 per cent and one-half of 1 per cent. In Scotland between 1921 and 1931 a small *decline* in population actually took place (of nearly 40,000 on the previous figure of 4,900,000 or so); while the intercensal rate of growth since 1931 has averaged only one quarter of 1 per cent or less annually.

The population trend in what is now Northern Ireland has been rather different. In censuses between 1821 and 1901 intercensal population increases only took place on three occasions, while *decreases* occurred in five instances. In that eighty-year period the population fell by 143,000 (from 1,380,000 to 1,237,000). In the sixty years since then the population has, however, risen by 188,000 (to 1,425,000), but the average annual rate of intercensal increase has been less than one quarter of 1 per cent until, at the 1961 Census, it rose to nearly one half of 1 per cent.

Fertility

4

Put in very general terms, and leaving migration out of account, the rate of growth of Great Britain's population in the century preceding the First World War was largely determined by declining mortality throughout the period, and deliberate family limitation from the 1860s onwards. From being a country of (by today's standards) high mortality and high fertility, we became one of low mortality and low fertility. We entered an era of small families and high life expectancy.

There is no difficulty in accounting for either of these developments. Better diet, improved hygiene, the advance of medical knowledge and its application, brought about continuous reductions in mortality rates, although in the case of the survival chances of infants significant improvements did not take place until very late in the period. On the fertility side, too, the lines of explanation are fairly clear. Knowledge of the means of family limitation had been spreading ever since the early part of the nineteenth century, and the Bradlaugh–Besant trials played their part in calling public attention to the matter. In the upper and middle-class circles where people began to have smaller families, there were many factors likely to create a favourable climate of opinion for such a development. The range of satisfactions considered appropriate for civilised existence was expanding rapidly, and habits of expenditure once adopted proved resistant to being given up when there was widespread alarm at the 'Great Depression' and its possible consequences. The new emphasis on education and specialised training as a means of preserving and if possible improving the social and economic position of one's children was another factor. And many other influences were at work, including the decline in religious belief, the spread of the scientific attitude of mind, the weakening of the family as an economic unit, the growth of urban living, and the emancipation of women. The fewer the children, the better the start in life that they could be given; and though this was no new discovery, much that was currently happening seemed to reinforce the lesson, not merely for the middle classes but also for those lower in the social scale to whom the fashion spread. The surveys of Charles Booth, and the long line of social investigators following him, brought out the close relationship between large families and poverty. Not only did wages take no account of family responsibilities, but the benefits of the new National Insurance Act of 1911 failed to do so either.

Small wonder, then, that as the means of voluntarily controlling the size of one's family became more and more readily available, the practice became ever more widely adopted. Not that the development was confined to this country; though some of the factors involved may have been peculiar to Britain, many were clearly common to Western society as a whole, and the trend towards the small family pattern, first noticed in early nineteenth-century France, was soon well established both in Europe and in the English-speaking areas of the New World.

It was not until the interwar period that public concern about the possible consequences for Britain of the general adoption of the small family pattern reached substantial proportions. Mounting anxiety about the likelihood of a declining population and its possible implications led eventually to the setting-up of a Royal Commission on Population in 1944. The special investigations conducted on the Commission's behalf, and the very valuable reports in which the results of these and of the Commission's own deliberations were recorded, did not entirely allay the anxieties. It seemed, on the best evidence available to the Commission, that an actual population decline (as distinct from a continuance of the declining *rate* of population growth to which we had become accustomed) was quite possible and, on balance, not to be welcomed. Efforts should be made to redress, at least in part, the financial disadvantages to which the heads of large families were subject; and emigration, except on an extremely modest scale, should in future be frowned upon. The one somewhat gloomy statistic capturing the popular imagination of that day was to the effect that, among the couples married in 1925–29, it was estimated that the ultimate mean number of children would probably be 2·2. The whole number might replace the parents, but the fraction, it was popularly believed, might well not replace the bachelors and spinsters. Fortunately, things did not turn out quite like this. And although everyone knew that we could not count upon a continuance of the postwar births 'bulge' of 1946 and 1947, we appeared *thereafter* to be settling down to annual numbers of births which gave us at least a modest safety margin. The danger of ultimately entering upon a population decline seemed, at least for the time, to have been postponed.

Looking back on our population history from the vantage point of the mid-1950s, the situation seemed fairly clear. We had experienced an almost continuous reduction in fertility ever since the late 1860s and this had been associated with the spread of voluntary family limitation. One way of showing the extent of this reduction in fertility was by looking at the decline in the mean ultimate family size of marriage cohorts. For the marriage cohorts of the 1860s, mean ultimate family size was a little over six; for the cohorts of the 1880s it declined to around five, while for those of the 1890s it was a little over four. The decline persisted until the position was reached that, for the cohorts of the late 1920s, it was a little over two. Although information was necessarily incomplete for later marriage cohorts than this, the evidence suggested that mean ultimate family size was likely to stabilise itself at this sort of level. There were, of course, fluctuations in the annual numbers of recorded births. The lowest point was reached in 1933, and annual numbers increased between then and the outbreak of war. After the Second World War an increase in births, associated with 'postponed' births and corresponding to a similar development after the First World War, took place. The 'bulge' of 1946 and 1947 was followed by a decline to a level somewhat above that of the immediate prewar years. Taken together with the trends in mortality and migration, the picture presented was that of a country whose population during the previous century or so had continued to grow steadily at a relatively slow and latterly slightly declining rate, but where the most recent evidence suggested that the dangers of an actual *decline* in population, which had been very much present in people's minds at the time of the Royal Commission on Population, had at least for the time being receded.

If this, then, was how things looked in retrospect in, say, 1955, the quite unexpected events of 1956 and the following years completely altered the picture. For in 1956 and all subsequent years up to and including 1964, every year showed a substantially greater number of births than the preceding one. In the five-year period 1956–60 live births in England and Wales were 9·8 per cent higher than they had been in the five-year period 1951–55. The differences between individual years were even more startling, the figure for 1964 being no less than 31·7 per cent higher than that for 1955. It was hardly surprising that a change of this order of magnitude should have led to a complete reassessment of the whole situation. In attempting to identify the constituent elements immediately involved in the continuous increase in annual births during this nine-year period, it must be remembered that the factors themselves, as well as the interrelationship between them, are extremely complex and that an over-simplified account of the type given here cannot be more than a brief and inadequate introduction.

Clearly, an increase in the number of married women was one of the factors involved in the nine-year increase in *legitimate* births. In a recent *Statistical Review* the Registrar General for England and Wales pointed out that 'marriage rates have been very high, and for the average spinster marriage prospects are about as high as they can be'. The change can be shown in striking form by the following figures. Of every thousand women in the age group 20 to 39 in England and Wales in 1911, 552 were married women. In 1931 the figure was 572, in 1951 it was 731 and in 1961 it had reached 808. Indeed, the married proportion of almost every age group has been growing and is continuing to grow. For both men and women in the age group 15 to 24 it had, in 1964, more than doubled since 1931. Another closely related tendency that has been at work is that towards marrying at younger ages. Though this had been observed from an even earlier period, it can be noted that the mean age at marriage of spinsters in England and Wales decreased from 25·54 in 1926–30 to 24·58 in 1941–45, 23·73 in 1956 and 23·03 in 1962. Another way of putting it is to say that nearly 29 per cent of spinster brides in 1961 were under 20 compared with only 11 per cent in 1938 and 10 per cent in 1931.

Apart from greater marriage intensity and more marriages, and the tendency to marry at younger ages, an increase in legitimate fertility attributable to other factors has evidently taken place. The Registrar General for England and Wales, reviewing the evidence for the period 1955 to 1962, said it had been one of 'generally buoyant fertility resulting from a factor or set of factors which have affected women of practically all ages and durations of marriage'. It is, of course, too early to be *certain* how all this (including the tendency to marry younger) will be reflected in the mean ultimate family size of the marriage cohorts of 1955 and later years; we cannot yet be sure of the position even for the earlier postwar cohorts. *Some* increase in ultimate family size is, however, expected to be shown when the marriage cohorts of these nine years have had time substantially to complete their family building.

Though nine births out of ten are still legitimate, it remains true that, in the period under consideration, the number of illegitimate births rose much more rapidly than did the number of legitimate births. A proportion of the 'boom in babies' of these years is therefore attributable to this factor. And it is to be remembered that this was happening at a time when the number of single women between 15 and 49 was shrinking as a result of the increasing tendency of women to marry. A final factor to which reference has to be made in accounting for the upward swing in births is that of immigration. At least during the first two-thirds of the period of this upward swing there was also a substantial increase in immigration, including immigration from the West Indies and other areas with higher fertility than our own. It has been officially suggested that as much as a quarter or even a third of the additional births of those years could be attributable to this immigration factor.

Although in the preceding paragraphs the 'boom in babies' has been spoken of as a phenomenon of the nine-year period 1956 to

1964, it is obviously too early to judge whether the downward tendency in annual numbers of births in 1965 and 1966 marks the beginning of a new phase or is merely a temporary halt in a secular upward trend. Control of immigration under the provisions of the Commonwealth Immigrants Act 1962 has, rightly or wrongly, greatly reduced the numbers coming in; and one factor in increasing annual numbers of births has therefore been held in check. To give only one other example of a further factor possibly making for a halt in the upswing of births, there is the special case of the babies in the 'bulge' years of 1946 and 1947 reaching marriageable ages. It is obvious that, as a result of the additional births of those years, more girls will be entering the younger marriageable age groups in the early 1960s than have hitherto been doing so or will be doing so subsequently. Of itself, this might be expected, at least temporarily, substantially to increase the number of annually-recorded births. However, traditionally in this country young women tend to marry young men who are on an average nearly three years older than they are. Consequently, when the first of the 'bulge' girls reach marriageable ages, the number of such young men available will be smaller than that of their female counterparts of three years younger, because these young men were born before the 'bulge' occurred. And this deficiency of bridegrooms the traditional amount older than their brides could be substantial. A few years later, when the 'bulge' *boys* begin to think of marrying, they are likely to find a corresponding shortage of brides the traditional amount *younger* than themselves. It is hard to predict what the outcome of this complex situation is likely to be in terms of annual numbers of births, but it could well disturb traditional patterns of marriage ages at least for a time.

Mortality 5

Infant mortality

Although there are many other indices, such as maternal mortality rates and still birth rates, which for certain purposes have special value, the infant mortality rate is widely accepted as an index of economic and social progress. This index can therefore be taken as an example of how things have developed in this country. From the middle of the nineteenth century to the beginning of the twentieth, the infant mortality rate (deaths of infants before their first birthday per thousand related live births) remained fairly constant at around 150. After the turn of the century, however, there began a long period of fairly continuous improvement up to the present time, with only temporary deteriorations due to the special circumstances of war. The failure of the rate to reflect medical progress and social improvement in the nineteenth century is generally attributed to the failure to apply the increased knowledge gained during that period. It seems that it was not until the midwifery service was statutorily recognised and progressively extended in the early part of the twentieth century, and until standards of hygiene were improved, that any improvement in the infant mortality rate could be achieved. The period of progress in reducing the infant mortality rate had to wait until accumulated knowledge could be practically applied; and thereafter advancing medical knowledge and its practical application jointly contributed towards the continuous decline in the rate. Before the outbreak of the Second World War the rate had been reduced to less than 53. During and after the war the introduction of penicillin and the development of effective vaccines brought spectacular improvements, and the rate fell to 32 in the late 1940s. From the mid

1950s, when the rate stood at about 23, to the mid 1960s by which it had fallen to 19, progress has slowed down somewhat; but it was still usually the case that the infant mortality rate for each quarter and for each year was a record by comparison with the corresponding preceding period.

Of the other countries of the British Isles, Scotland has, since the end of the first decade of the present century, always had a higher mortality rate than that of England and Wales; in 1964 it stood at 24·1 by comparison with 20. Northern Ireland at the same date had a rate of 26·5, and Eire one of 26·8. The general trend of infant mortality rates in the United States and in the Scandinavian countries has been broadly similar to that of England and Wales, but in recent years we have lagged behind Sweden (13·6) the Netherlands (15·8) and Norway and Denmark (18·7), though maintaining our lead over France (23·4) and Italy (35·5). If we break infant deaths down into those occurring in the first four weeks after birth (neonatal deaths), and those from the fifth week to the first birthday (postneonatal deaths), a 90 per cent reduction has been achieved in the latter since the early part of this century as against only a 60 per cent reduction in the former. The control of infectious diseases has been more successful than has the control of congenital malformations and other causes of death particularly serious in the early weeks of life.

Expectation of life

A convenient way of summarising the mortality experience of all age groups of a population is provided by figures of life expectancy at birth for the two sexes. Such figures show, for live born baby boys and baby girls respectively, the average future lifetime they could expect to have if they were subjected throughout their lives to the recorded age and sex death rates of the period at which they were born. Since mortality rates are in fact decreasing almost universally, in all countries, life expectancy figures calculated on this basis tend to understate the true expectation of life, since they assume a continuance of the current mortality rates. The usefulness of life expectancy figures for showing how the situation has improved in a particular country over time, and for comparing the position in different countries at the same point in time is not, of course, in any way reduced by this circumstance, since all the figures are understatements and have been calculated on a broadly similar basis.

Taking England and Wales to represent the situation in Britain, life expectancy for new born boys and girls has risen from 40 and 42 in the mid-nineteenth century to $48\frac{1}{2}$ and $52\frac{1}{2}$ in the first decade of the present century; it stood at around 59 and 63 in the early 1930s, had improved to $66\frac{1}{2}$ and $71\frac{1}{2}$ in the early 1950s, and now, in the early 1960s, is very nearly 68 and 74. Similar developments in Scotland and Northern Ireland have led up to the current expectancy in those countries of 66 and 72 in Scotland and $67\frac{1}{2}$ and $72\frac{1}{2}$ in Northern Ireland.

In terms of current life expectancy at birth, Britain ranks high amongst the nations of the world, with figures very similar to those in Australia and New Zealand, in the United States and in France, but somewhat below those in Sweden, Norway and the Netherlands (71 and 75), and Denmark (70 and 74). It will be noticed that the sex differential has widened in England and Wales, from two years to six; the current sex differential for the other countries mentioned earlier varies between three and a half and seven years. In almost every country the differential takes the form that girls have a longer life expectancy than boys; in recent years the only countries where this situation has been reversed have been Ceylon and India (though in the latter country the more usual differential has recently emerged). The main factors responsible for the improved expectation of life in Britain over the last century or so are well known, and they include improved dietary, rising standards of living, increased medical knowledge and the increasing application of that knowledge through the provision of better medical and health facilities to wider sections of the population, and better working conditions, together with the transition from the large to the small family pattern, which has enabled mothers to look after their children more effectively. Naturally, these factors have been of varying importance at different times during the last hundred years, and their effectiveness in reducing mortality has varied as between the different age groups and the two sexes. The broad picture is that, by comparison with our counterparts of earlier generations, many more of us are surviving to the fifties, sixties and seventies. Chances of survival to the eighties and nineties have not, however, shown corresponding improvements. The further expectation of life of women of 75, for example, was a little more than six and a half years in 1841–45, and has only risen to a little over eight and a half years in 1956–60.

It may be that we have now passed the point at which further advances in hygiene and in diets can produce substantial reductions in mortality. It certainly seems as though the most recent improvements in life expectancy have been due in the main to the growth of medical knowledge and the availability of medical services. Future increases in life expectancy would seem more likely to result from further changes of this kind.

Sex differences in mortality

Although this question has been touched upon already, it deserves somewhat fuller treatment at this point. At the present time about 106 boys are born for every 100 girls in England and Wales. There is, of course, no necessary permanence about this particular ratio. The experience of our own and other countries has shown that the ratio of the births of boys to the births of girls tends to rise in the closing stages of wars and shortly afterwards. Why this should be so is still obscure, though it might have something to do with another feature of the same kind of period, the tendency of the proportion of first and second children to rise at such times and for the father's age to fall. At all events, the ratio has risen from 104 in the years before the First World War to 105 in the early 1930s and 106 since the mid-1940s.

This disparity in the numbers of the two sexes at birth is steadily reduced in subsequent years by contrary tendencies making for slightly greater mortality at all ages amongst boys than amongst girls. The male disadvantage in infancy and childhood used, it is true, to be greater than it is now; but some difference still remains. In 1911 the relatively greater difficulty of rearing boys as compared with girls meant that parity of numbers between the two sexes came about by the age of 10. In 1963, however, parity of numbers is only reached at the age of 42, though differential mortality is not the only factor involved in this striking difference. At older ages the death rates for men have in recent years fallen much less than for women, with the result that the extent to which women outnumber men in these older age groups has been increasing. The increase that has taken place in a comparatively short time can be seen by taking the age group 75 and over. In the 1951 Census there were in this age group 620 men to every 1000 women; by 1963 there were nearly twice as many women as there were men.

Another way of looking at it is to take the ratio of men to women in the age group 15 to 44. In England and Wales in 1921 there were 876 men to every 1,000 women in this age group, and the figure rose to 915 in 1931, 969 in 1951 and 1,028 in 1965. The main factors bringing about this startling change in the ratio between the sexes in this marriageable age group have included two that we have already mentioned, namely the increased proportion of males to females at birth and the improvement in male infant and child mortality relative to female mortality. The other factors appear to have been first, the non-recurrence of the heavy mortality amongst men in the First World War, and secondly, the reduction of the male preponderance amongst emigrants. This elimination of the so-called 'surplus of women' in the marriageable age groups, of which we used to hear so much in the interwar period, has clearly had far-reaching social consequences. It has certainly been one factor in the change in the proportion of *married* women in the younger age group when the prewar is compared with the postwar period. Of women aged 20 to 24 in England and Wales in 1931 only about a quarter were married, whereas in 1951 the proportion had risen to nearly a half.

Immigration and emigration

It is well-known that from the beginning of the nineteenth century until the 1930s there was a very substantial net outward movement of population from this country. It is estimated that in this period the number of people leaving Britain for destinations outside Europe, mainly in the Commonwealth and the United States, considerably exceeded 20 million. Some of these emigrants, of course, returned later; and considerable numbers of Europeans came to Britain. The net flow was certainly in an outward direction, though figures as to its extent are unreliable for the early period. It is estimated that the net loss by migration from the present area of the United Kingdom amounted to some 4 million between 1871 and 1931. Between the same dates England and Wales is estimated to have sustained a net loss by migration of over 2 million. Scotland and Northern Ireland continued throughout the period to have a net outward movement of population to countries overseas as well as to England and Wales. One way of putting all this is to say that, during this very long era of net outward movement, all the constituent countries of what is now the United Kingdom were cushioned against the full impact of the natural increase (i.e. excess of births over deaths) of their populations by the effects of migration. From the 1930s to the outbreak of war a significant change in previous migration trends took place. A net inflow replaced the long-standing net outflow, and this change was due partly to the fact that the Dominions no longer wanted immigrants for a time after the onset of the World economic crisis, partly to a steep rise in the number of returning emigrants, and partly to extensive immigration of refugees from the Continent.

During the war itself emigration virtually ceased, and no one could clearly foresee the new pattern of migration that would establish itself once the war was over. In the first ten years or so after the war we experienced a net loss by migration, though it was small both by comparison with our population size and when viewed alongside the figures of the period before the 1930s. So although it looked at first as though the traditional pattern of migration had re-established itself, it was certainly not on the traditional scale. Indeed, between the Census of 1931 and that of 1951 (no census having been taken in 1941), England and Wales retained its full natural increase plus a net gain of three-quarters of a million or so by migration from elsewhere (partly, of course, from Scotland and from Northern Ireland and Eire). And despite the postwar outward balances, there was a net gain by migration between these census dates for the United Kingdom as a whole of about half a million, or an average of 25,000 a year. In the following ten years (1951–61) the United Kingdom again experienced a net gain by migration, though on a more modest scale (averaging some 9,700 a year). The gross movements underlying this relatively small inward balance are believed, however, to have been quite large. Thus emigration from the United Kingdom to the Commonwealth probably reached 200,000 or more in each of the peak years 1952 and 1957, and immigration from Eire, from elsewhere in the Commonwealth, and from Europe was correspondingly large. This immigration, particularly from Commonwealth countries such as the West Indies and Pakistan, increased so substantially that, from 1958 onwards, the shortlived postwar period of net outward migration balances from the United Kingdom was replaced by one of relatively large net *inward* balances—in the five years 1958–62 these amounted to 45,000, 44,000, 82,000, 172,000 and 136,000 respectively. By the end of this five-year period, however, the Commonwealth Immigrants Act 1962 had empowered the Government to restrict the number of persons from the Commonwealth (and, in principle, Eire) who might immigrate into the United Kingdom without assured prospects of employment or adequate means of self-support, and to deport unsuitable immigrants. The last-minute flood of immigrants just before the Act came into force on 1 July 1962 was reflected in the high net inward balance of that year; in the following year (1963) this balance had fallen to only

10,000. This was the last year showing a net inward movement to the United Kingdom. In 1964 and in the two subsequent years there have been *outward* balances on an ascending scale, starting at 17,000 and rising, it would appear, to over twice, and then to over three times that figure.

In all this, the United Kingdom figures rather tend to mask what was happening in the constituent countries, and even indirectly what was happening in relation to Eire. In very general terms, England and Wales experienced a net gain by migration from Scotland and Northern Ireland in the 1950s of about 20,000 a year, and from Eire of about 25,000 a year. In the five years mid-1960 to mid-1964 England and Wales experienced an annual average net gain by migration to and from Eire of 31,000; and of 30,000 in relation to Scotland and Northern Ireland combined. She experienced in those years very large net gains by migrants with foreign or overseas Commonwealth countries' passports, this gain amounting to some 124,000 a year during the period. The net *outflow* of migrants with United Kingdom passports going beyond the United Kingdom and Eire amounted to some 62,000 a year. Putting all these net inflow and net outflow figures together, the combined effect was to produce a net inward migration balance for England and Wales averaging 119,000 annually during this five-year period.

Everyone connected with either the compilation or the use of British migration figures had for many years been acutely aware of how unsatisfactory the basic data were. A major gap related to those travelling by air, who did not figure in migration data at all; and in other respects also, complex 'marrying' of material from different sources had to be engaged in to produce even approximate estimates of the extent and direction of movement. Accordingly, it was eventually arranged that the Social Survey (Central Office of Information) should, on behalf of the Board of Trade, interview on a voluntary basis a stratified random sample of passengers entering and leaving the United Kingdom on all the principal air and sea routes (other than from and to Eire) to obtain information about international migration, tourism, and the contribution of 'travel' expenditure to the international balance of payments. The sampling fraction varies from one type of traffic to another, and was never intended to be large enough for reliability in dealing with relatively small sub-groups of migrants. From 1 January 1964 onwards many official migration figures previously based only on movement by the long sea routes have been discontinued and replaced by statistics derived from this sample International Passenger Survey, which had been gradually building up since 1961. Though this is clearly to be welcomed, it means that strict comparability between many of the figures for 1964 and later years on the one hand and those relating to 1963 and earlier years on the other, has had to be sacrificed.

The latest available figures based on this International Passenger Survey are, at the time of writing, for 1965. It should be remembered that they relate to a declared *intention* by the passenger to reside in or leave the country for at least a year, whereas some of the figures quoted earlier have been adjusted for subsequent changes of intention. It should also be noted that traffic between Eire and the United Kingdom is not included. Bearing these points in mind, it seems that some 224,800 British citizens left the United Kingdom in 1965, while 76,000 came in, leaving an outward balance of 148,500. Some 72,600 Commonwealth citizens entered the United Kingdom, and 33,000 left, producing an inward balance of 39,600. Amongst citizens of other countries, immigrants (70,200) predominated; those leaving numbered 36,100, so that the inward balance was 34,100. The combined effect of these movements was that emigrants (293,900) exceeded immigrants (219,100), and the overall outward balance amounted to 74,700.

Again excluding movement between the United Kingdom and Eire, where did these emigrants, whatever their citizenship, go to in 1965? Nearly a third went to Australia, about 15 per cent to Canada, and 5 or 6 per cent each to New Zealand and to the African countries of the Commonwealth combined. A further 9 per cent went elsewhere in the Commonwealth, making the Commonwealth the destination of over two-thirds of all emigrants from the United Kingdom. South Africa accounted for a further 4 per cent. The United States attracted 10 per cent, and western Europe 15 per cent, leaving only about 4 per cent for all other non-Commonwealth countries combined.

In the case of immigrants into the United Kingdom (and still excluding movement between Eire and the United Kingdom), the Commonwealth accounts for over half the total. About 11 per cent came from India, Pakistan and Ceylon, 10 per cent from the African countries of the Commonwealth, 9 per cent from Australia, nearly 9 per cent from the West Indies, 5 per cent from Canada, 3 per cent from New Zealand and nearly 8 per cent from the remainder of the Commonwealth. Western Europe was the origin of 27 per cent of the total, the United States of 10 per cent, South Africa of 2 per cent, leaving about 6 per cent for all other non-Commonwealth countries combined. This pattern of origin is, of course, very different from that obtaining before the Commonwealth Immigrants Act 1962 came into operation.

How far do those currently moving into and out of the United Kingdom (again excluding movement between Eire and the United Kingdom) differ substantially in such respects as sex, age and broad occupational category? Of those emigrating from the United Kingdom in 1965, just over half were males; amongst immigrants, males formed nearly 49 per cent of the total. Amongst the emigrants, 24 per cent were under 15 and 2 per cent over 65, while amongst those immigrating the corresponding proportions were 19 per cent and 2 per cent. The proportion in the 15–24 age group was, however, considerably higher in the case of immigrants (37 per cent) than in that of emigrants (27 per cent); in that sense, the working-age population we are receiving is younger than the one we are losing. Broad occupational categories are notoriously unsatisfactory, but those who classified themselves as 'administrators, managers and persons with professional and technological qualifications' constituted similar proportions of the total amongst both immigrants (19 per cent) and emigrants (16 per cent). Because of the greater *number* of emigrants this still, of course, meant a net loss of such people amounting to perhaps 5,000.

It is in some ways more meaningful to restrict the comparison to specific types of skill. The difficulties in providing a true picture of what is happening can be illustrated by taking the case of qualified medical practitioners. It is obvious that many students from overseas come to this country to obtain a medical training, and that some of them subsequently return to their own countries as qualified doctors, while others remain here either temporarily or permanently. It is also clear that British doctors go overseas, for further training or experience or for preference, in substantial numbers. Published figures showing the net result of these movements are difficult to interpret and sometimes contradictory, but in a House of Commons debate on 13 February 1967 the Minister of Technology said that our loss of doctors through emigration amounted to between 300 and 350 a year, though the figure at the moment could be nearer 400. How serious in its implications was a loss on this scale? Set against a background of some 60,000 civilian doctors in Britain, expansion of our medical schools and improved pay and conditions, this annual rate of loss might not seem alarming. Yet in any one year this figure represents a high proportion of the medical school output, and against a background of a downward trend in the number of General Medical Practitioners and an upward trend in the general population, the position looks much less favourable.

Better figures, to clarify the nature and extent of the 'brain drain' as a whole, were promised in the same debate, through the setting-up of an interdepartmental committee on emigration statistics under the auspices of the General Register Office. In addition, the first report of a group under the chairmanship of Dr F. E. Jones, Managing Director of Mullards, engaged in studying, *inter alia*, the statistics and economics of emigration, was due in May 1967. This news was particularly welcome in view of figures previously published by the Society of British Aerospace Companies suggesting, on the basis of a 70 per cent response to a questionnaire sent to 436 member firms, that in 1966 as many as 1,300 'qualified specialists' left that industry for 'foreign employment'; of this number, 520 were said to have gone to the United States, 344 to foreign firms in Britain, 216 to Canada, and 125 to Australia, smaller numbers going to South Africa and to Europe. These, of course, are not official figures; they do not in all cases involve actual movement overseas, and the definition of a 'qualified specialist' does not necessarily correspond to the categories used elsewhere. The *basis* on which many official migration figures now rest, however, the International Passenger Survey, does not, because of sampling and other limitations, enable data to be published at present for small but important groups such as nuclear physicists.

The changing proportion of the England and Wales population born elsewhere reflects the changing volume of immigration during the last half century. At the time of the 1931 Census slightly less than 1 per cent of the England and Wales population had been born in Scotland, and a similar proportion had been born in Ireland. By the 1961 Census the Scottish-born proportion had risen to nearly $1\frac{1}{2}$ per cent, and the Irish-born to nearly 2 per cent. In 1931 at least 1·3 per cent, and perhaps as many as 1·7 per cent (depending on how we treat those whose birthplace was unstated) of the England and Wales population had been born outside the British Isles; by 1961 this figure had risen to 3·1 per cent, and the number was over 1,400,000.

In view of the relatively large number of overseas Commonwealth immigrants coming to this country since the mid-1950s, it is not surprising that a special set of tables relating to Commonwealth immigrants in the conurbations should have been produced out of the 1961 England and Wales Census material, based on a 10 per cent sample. The tables relate to persons born in specified Commonwealth countries and Colonial territories who were found at the time of the Census to be resident in one or other of six conurbations. In all, there were some 255,000 such immigrants, of whom 58 per cent were males. Of these over three-quarters went to the Greater London Conurbation, 12 per cent to the West Midlands Conurbation, 5 per cent and $4\frac{1}{2}$ per cent to the Conurbations of West Yorkshire and South-East Lancashire respectively, and 2 per cent and 1 per cent to the Merseyside and Tyneside Conurbations. In proportion to the relative size of these conurbations, Greater London got very much more than its share of these immigrants, the West Midlands Conurbation attracted only slightly less than its relative share, the West Yorkshire Conurbation only received about half the 'expected' proportion, and the remaining three conurbations, one-third or less of the proportion their relative populations might have suggested. It can be seen that, in general, the ratio between the actual and the expected proportion of these Commonwealth immigrants going to each of the six conurbations in England and Wales *decreases* as the distance of the conurbation from the Metropolis *increases*.

Taking these Commonwealth immigrants to the six conurbations, over a third had been born in the continent of India (30 per cent in India, 6 per cent in Pakistan). About two-fifths had been born in the British Caribbean (24·7 per cent in Jamaica, 16·3 per cent elsewhere). The next largest group (14·5 per cent) consisted of those born in Cyprus or Malta; and the contribution of the African continent (excluding the Republic of South Africa) was the smallest of all (8·5 per cent).

Another immigration question on which recent Census figures shed some light is the extent to which immigrants tend to live under more crowded conditions than the rest of the population. Census results in this matter are expressed in terms of the 'household', defined as 'a person living alone or a group living together, eating meals prepared together and benefiting by a common housekeeping'. If we take the density of $1\frac{1}{2}$ persons per room, then only 2·6 per cent of all England and Wales households were living at or above that density in 1961. The corresponding figure for *immigrant* households was 9·6 per cent; and for those where the main breadwinner was born in the Caribbean it was as high as 37·3 per cent. The average density at which the households in the Caribbean immigrant group were living was 1·22 people per room, compared with an average for all England and Wales households of 0·66.

It should, of course, be remembered that the figures just discussed only relate to those who had come to this country before the 1961 Census was taken. What the Registrar General calls 'the really significant intake of immigrants from the new Commonwealth countries' took place, however, in the fifteen months *after* the 1961 Census and to a smaller extent since then. Unofficial but reliable estimates of the size and distribution of the coloured population within Great Britain identify the Greater London Conurbation as having the largest absolute number (perhaps 350,000, representing 4 per cent of the Conurbation's population, two-thirds of them West

Indians but also a substantial contingent of Indians), followed by Birmingham (perhaps 70,000, or 6 per cent of the town's population, two-thirds West Indians, most of the remainder from India and Pakistan), Nottingham (perhaps 12,000, or 4 per cent of the towns-people, mostly West Indians), Bradford (a similar number, again forming about 4 per cent of the town's population, but this time mostly Pakistanis), Manchester and Liverpool (perhaps 10,000 each, the former mostly West Indians, the latter very mixed as to area of origin). Other towns with between 6,000 and 7,000 apiece are Wolverhampton, Leeds, Coventry, Huddersfield, Bristol, Leicester and Sheffield. Smaller absolute numbers, though sometimes fórming a higher proportion of the town's population, have settled in West Bromwich (about 6 per cent), Dudley, Bedford and High Wycombe (in each of these three cases probably forming at least 8 per cent of the townspeople), Newcastle upon Tyne, Slough and Smethwick. It seems unlikely that any of the other urban areas of Great Britain has at present more than 4,000 coloured people, or as high a coloured proportion of its population as the 4 to 8 per cent quoted in some of the cases mentioned earlier.

c

It is a commonplace that Britain's population is, and has been for a long time, predominantly urban and suburban; that a rural way of life in the sense to be found in many other countries is virtually absent in this country. The drift from the countryside to the towns, from agriculture to industry, was taking place all during the nineteenth century and had, by the end of that century, already created a situation in which three-quarters of the population was urban-living. By 1961 only 4 per cent of the working population was engaged in agriculture; and though some 20 per cent of the population lived in areas classed administratively as 'rural' (e.g. in Rural Districts), very many of these were either living on the fringes of towns or in towns not yet quite ready to be raised to the status of Urban Districts, or working and shopping and seeking their entertainment in urban areas even if not actually living in them.

Not merely have urban areas gained population at the expense of rural ones, but the larger urban areas have (at least until recently) gained at the expense of the smaller ones. The censuses of England and Wales and of Scotland (and the periodic estimates of population) now give figures for seven 'conurbations', which consist of continuously built-up, economically interdependent areas, and include developing suburbs of the towns within them. One of these (the Central Clydeside Conurbation) is in Scotland; the remaining six are in England, ranging in order of population size from Greater London, South-East Lancashire, West Midlands, West Yorkshire, and Merseyside to Tyneside. Between them these seven large urban agglomerations account for well over a third of the population of Great Britain. Several cities not far short of half a million in population size, and with important adjacent urban areas, have not yet been classed as conurbations for census purposes. If the populations of these near-conurbations (centring on Sheffield, Edinburgh and Bristol) were grouped with those of the seven already classified in that way, their combined population would certainly exceed two-fifths of the Great Britain total.

A whole host of factors, natural and man-made, have contributed towards the uneven distribution of the population. Many attempts have been made to describe this uneven distribution in words. It can be pointed out, for example, that a coffin-like central area, 60 or 65 miles wide and 200 miles long, stretching from the mouth of the Thames to the mouth of the Mersey, contains some 30 million of Great Britain's 52 million people, and includes five of the seven conurbations and one of the three 'near-conurbations'. When all is said and done, however, no verbal description can really be a substitute for a map showing varying population density by administrative areas. Such maps, particularly if their scale is large, if the administrative areas used are the smallest for which separate figures are available, and if the density categories distinguished are numerous, can show significant intercensal changes in the spatial distribution of population. They show, for instance, the extent to which in some areas a process of 'urban dispersal' has been taking place. In the Greater London Conurbation, for example, there had been for a long time a tendency for fewer people to live in the central area, but this was balanced by the movement of people to the suburbs and beyond, both from the central area and from outside the conurbation. The growth of the suburban and outer suburban areas was in some respects retarded by the Second World War, and both the inner area (where the County of London's population fell by 800,000 people or so) and the conurbation as a whole, experienced net losses between 1939 and 1951. The spread of car ownership and other factors have been associated with a still further fall between then and now in the population of the inner area; the population of the conurbation *outside* London County has changed comparatively little; and the area *beyond* the conurbation has experienced almost continuous population increase. Much of this is beyond the Green Belt but still within what one can loosely describe as the London 'region', a circular area with a radius of 40–50 miles from the centre and an overall population increase of perhaps half a million since 1951. This redistribution of people has been partly planned and partly unplanned. It has taken the form both of the planned dispersal of population and industry from congested areas of old London to New Towns and other deliberately expanded small towns encouraged to take some of London's 'overspill', and also of population movement which the authorities were unable or unwilling to prevent, where the breadwinners continued to work in inner London but 'commuted' to and from their work places despite the cost of the travel in time and money.

Urban dispersal of both these types has, of course, also taken place in many other areas on an important scale. The centres of many large cities, and sometimes also the whole city and the conurbation of which it forms part, have remained static or declined in population, while the more desirable areas within possible daily travelling distance, or to which employment opportunities have moved, have gained at their expense. Though this may take the form of a reversal of the traditional drift from the surrounding countryside to the town, it clearly in no sense arrests, but rather accentuates, the long-standing process of replacing a rural by an urban way of life.

The drift from the villages to the towns, and the drift from the central and inner areas of a town to the outer areas and beyond (at least so far as it was unplanned) were often deplored. So was the drift from the older areas of industrial development and mineral exploitation in Scotland, Northern England and Wales to other parts of England, particularly the Midlands and the South East. Indeed, so serious a view was taken of the possible economic and social consequences of this long-standing drift to the South that a Royal Commission on the Distribution of the Industrial Population was, in the late 1930s, set up to examine the whole problem. Ever since then Governments, with varying degrees of enthusiasm and success, have been pursuing a policy of encouraging the establishment of new industrial opportunities in the regions from which population has traditionally been moving away, and restricting development in the magnetic regions in order to bring about a reversal of this trend and restore a better 'balance', economically and otherwise, between the different regions of the country. It is an indication of how seriously the latest planning of this kind (by the newly created Regional Economic Planning Councils and Boards) is taken in official circles, that regional population projections now take official account, at least to some degree, of the proposals for the future which are embodied in the published plans of these bodies.

Turning from types of internal migration to types of statistical data relating to internal migration, it had always been the practice to derive net migration figures for areas within England and Wales by combining the known facts of births and deaths in a particular district between census dates with the change in the enumerated population. Amongst the many disadvantages of relying on data of this type was the fact that no indication could be obtained in this way of the gross movements in opposite directions which the residual net movement represented. For any net movement of a given size could obviously have been the result of relatively small or of relatively large gross movements in opposite directions. When rationing was in operation it became possible to use the data relating to recorded changes of address for ration book purposes to throw some light on the extent and direction of internal migration. Studies made for the General Register Office in England and Wales suggested that very substantial movements of population were taking place. It seemed that even those areas in which for many years past a net outward movement had taken place, in fact experienced a substantial movement in *both* directions. The same was also apparently true of areas showing substantial net gains by migration. The County Borough of Watford, for example, though growing rapidly by inward movement, also experienced a substantial though smaller outward movement. One moral seemed to be that the planners of New Towns need not worry unduly if some of the families encouraged to go there should subsequently decide to leave, since this would only be in line with what was happening in the unplanned growth of most expanding urban areas.

The 1961 Census broke new ground by including a question to the 10 per cent sample on change of usual address. It thus became possible to identify as a 'migrant' anyone whose usual address on 23 April 1961 was different from their usual address on 23 April 1960, intermediate changes of address being ignored. On this basis, entirely new sets of tables have been provided for the first time. And although the population movement of one year, 1960–61, does not necessarily represent longer term trends, we are obviously in a much better position to examine the internal migration situation since this data became available than we were before.

A good deal can be learned from the tabulations relating to the ten standard regions (old style) and six conurbations of England and Wales. In Table 3 a net migration balance is shown for each of these areas, the net number of migrants into or out of the area being expressed as a proportion per thousand residents. The migration balances are very much what one would expect. Thus the regions with large *inward* migration balances relative to their population size are the Eastern, Southern and South Western Regions. Still with substantial inward balances, though not on the same scale, are the London and South Eastern, North Midland and Midland Regions. Relative favourable balances of half their size or less are found in the North Western and East and West Ridings Regions; while Wales and the Northern Region show the smallest favourable balances of all. Amongst the conurbations, Tyneside shows a large net *outward* balance, and Merseyside a fairly substantial one. The West Midlands and South-East Lancashire Conurbations show no balance either way. The Greater London Conurbation shows a small net inward balance and the West Yorkshire one a larger proportionate inward balance.

It is of some interest to compare this picture of the net 1960–61 migration per thousand population for each of the standard regions (old style) with similar ratios based on the Registrar General's estimated annual net internal plus external migration movements into or out of these regions over the periods 1951–61 and 1959–64 combined. Taking a mean of his combined absolute figures, and relating it to the 1963 populations of these regions, the South Western shows the largest relative inward migration balance (+ 5), followed by the Eastern, Southern, and London and South Eastern Regions combined ($+4$). The next most successful regions in attracting population are the Midland and North Midland ($+2\frac{1}{2}$ in each case). The *least* successful in this respect are the East and West Ridings and

TABLE 3

Migration balance, expressed as a proportion per thousand residents, of the net inward ($+$) or outward ($-$) population movement in tl˙ year 1960–61 (based on 10 per cent sample)

Standard Regions (Old) and Conurbations	Migration balance
Northern Region	$+1$
Tyneside Conurbation	-7
Remainder of Region	$+3$
East and West Ridings Region	$+2$
West Yorkshire Conurbation	$+3$
Remainder of Region	0
North Western Region	$+3$
South-East Lancashire Conurbation	0
Merseyside Conurbation	-4
Remainder of Region	$+9$
North Midland Region	$+7$
Midland Region	$+6$
West Midlands Conurbation	0
Remainder of Region	$+11$
Eastern Region	$+20$
London and South Eastern Region	$+7$
Greater London Conurbation	$+1$
Remainder of Region	$+23$
Southern Region	$+21$
South Western Region	$+13$
Wales	$+1$

Source. Census 1961, England and Wales.

North Regions (-2 in each case), with the North Western Region ($-1\frac{1}{2}$) and Wales (-1) also, on balance, losing population by migration, though on a relatively smaller scale.

The Registrar General's latest estimates of internal migration are for mid-1965 to mid-1966, and are given in terms of *revised* standard regions. These estimates suggest that currently the areas gaining by migration are the South West, East Anglia, East Midland and West Midland Regions, the largest drift from the rest of England and Wales being to the first two of these. Wales and the South East are neither gaining nor losing population by migration. In the case of Wales, a net inward traffic with England is counterbalanced by a net outward movement elsewhere. In the case of the South East Region, a substantial net *loss* by migration to the rest of England and Wales (showing how the traditional drift to the south-east has recently been replaced by a contrary tendency) is counterbalanced by a net inward movement from elsewhere. The areas with a net outflow of population are the Yorkshire and Humberside, North West and North Regions.

As explained above, however, the main merit of the new type of migration data provided in the 1961 Census lies in enabling us to see the gross movements which these net movements represent. In Table 4 the Tyneside Conurbation is taken as an example to show a particular area's migration balance-sheet with the rest of England and Wales. Southerners probably tend to think of the Tyneside Conurbation as an area which people move away from rather than into, and this is borne out by the migration balance figures we have already looked at. Table 4 makes it clear, however, that there was also a substantial movement *inwards* to the Tyneside Conurbation from every region of England and Wales to which Tynesiders went in 1960–61. Another interesting point to emerge from this example is the extent to which short distance moves contribute to the total number of moves. Of the Tyneside Conurbation men who changed their addresses between the specified dates in 1960 and 1961, 52·7 per cent were only moving to somewhere outside the conurbation but still within the Northern Region. Similarly, of those who acquired an address in the Tyneside Conurbation between those dates, no fewer than 46·1 per cent had only moved there from an address within the Northern Region. Where the attraction is strong enough, however, long-distance moves become numerically important as well. Thus in the Tyneside Conurbation case, 12·1 per cent of the male emigrants went to the London and South Eastern Region.

This leads to another important question. Where did the people come from who flocked to the areas attracting the largest absolute numbers of immigrants? If we take the London and South Eastern

TABLE 4

Emigration and immigration of males from and to the Tyneside Conurbation to and from the rest of England and Wales in the year 1960–61 (based on 10 per cent sample)

To or from	Male emigrants from Tyneside Conurbation to:	Male immigrants to Tyneside Conurbation from:
Remainder of Northern Region	5,180	2,620
East and West Ridings Region	490	550
North Western Region	540	390
North Midland Region	500	340
Midland Region	530	290
Eastern Region	470	270
London and South Eastern Region	1,190	690
Southern Region	450	180
South Western Region	350	250
Wales	120	100
Remainder of England and Wales as a whole	9,820	5,680

Source. Census 1961, England and Wales.
Note. Sample numbers have been 'grossed up'.

Region as our example, and examine the origin of male immigrants in terms of movement from abroad and from elsewhere in the British Isles as well as from the other regions of England and Wales, some interesting results emerge. Overseas countries accounted for 36·3 per cent of the net inward movement in 1960–61, and other parts of the British Isles for 13·2 per cent. Amongst the regions, the largest contribution came from the Eastern Region (12·3 per cent) and the next largest from the Southern Region (10·9 per cent). The South Western Region made a contribution of 6·4 per cent and the North Western of 5 per cent. Immigrants from the Midland and North

Midland Regions accounted for 3·9 per cent and 3·6 per cent of the total respectively, leaving the Northern Region only contributing 3 per cent, and Wales and the East and West Ridings 2·7 per cent each. Though the attraction of moving to the London and South Eastern Region certainly induced substantial population movements from all these areas, the relative importance of the contribution from the areas traditionally associated with the drift to the South East was comparatively small.

As a final example of where the immigrants to areas of high attraction came from, we may take the case of the West Midlands Conurbation. Of the male immigrants to that conurbation, 20·2 per cent came from abroad and 18·2 per cent from elsewhere in the British Isles than England and Wales. A similar proportion (20·9 per cent) came from the remainder of the Midland Region. No other region contributed as much as 5 per cent of the total; but three regions, Wales, the North Midland and the North Western Regions, contributed not far short of that percentage (4·9, 4·8 and 4·7). The Southern and South Western Regions contributed a little over 4 per cent each and the Eastern and East and West Ridings Regions a little over 3 per cent each, leaving only 2 per cent for the Northern Region.

Social class variations in mortality and fertility

Since the early part of the present century the Registrar General has, in presenting data relating to each population census, included a special category described as Social Class. For this purpose occupations have all been assigned to one of five Social Class Groups. Social Class I consists of high-status professional and business occupations; II includes such occupations as farming and teaching; III brings together a large number of skilled occupations both non-manual and manual; while IV and V are mainly composed of manual occupations, the former semi-skilled and the latter unskilled. Changes in the allocation of occupations to these five categories have taken place between censuses, but the broad pattern has remained the same. With all their faults (and since the last war they have been supplemented by a more sophisticated breakdown into three times this number of socio-economic groups), the Registrar General's five Social Classes have come to play a vital part in the analysis of demographic data. In particular, the census populations of adult males in each of these categories have been translated into appropriate 'populations at risk' in order to compare death registration figures for the different social class groups, since occupation (of the father in registering children's deaths, and of the subject in registering adult deaths) is recorded at the time of registration. This 'marrying' of populations at risk derived from a census with data derived from registration is not a straightforward operation, and can usually only be done for periods very close to a census date. This is why official figures of mortality by social class are not issued with the same regularity as are the death registration figures themselves.

Infant mortality by social class

Between 1911 (when mortality by social class was first estimated) and 1951 (the latest year for which in England and Wales the results of 'marrying' census and registration data have been published so far) the relative infant mortality of the social class groups has remained fairly constant, though there was, as we have already seen, a very large *overall* reduction in such mortality during this period. Step by step, as one descends the social scale, infant mortality rises. The magnitude of the differential can be indicated by the fact that, in Social Class V, the infant mortality rate has tended to be two or two and a half times as high as in Social Class I. Another way of putting it is to say that the rate for infants born into the families of unskilled labourers lags some thirty years behind that for those with fathers in the leading professions.

It is natural to ask what are the main factors involved in this social class gradient in infant mortality. Very many investigations in recent years have thrown light on this problem. Dr J. W. B. Douglas, in his pioneer following-up of a national sample of children born in the first week of March 1946, found that higher infant mortality at the lower end of the social scale was partly due to the higher incidence of premature births, which in its turn was associated with early childbearing, closely-spaced births, poor antenatal care, and excessive work (at home or factory) during the last months of pregnancy. He also found greater mortality in the postneonatal period (from four weeks to twelve months after birth) due to greater risk of death from infections such as bronchitis, pneumonia and gastro-enteritis, which in turn was associated with more crowded living conditions and larger families. He showed how, though the children of all social classes might expect to contract at least some of the typical infections of childhood at some time, those in overcrowded homes with several brothers and sisters were more likely to contract them early in life when the risk of their being fatal was greatest. Other investigators have confirmed that the social class gradient has hitherto proved equally marked in neonatal (birth to four weeks) and postneonatal deaths.

In explaining the persistence of this social class gradient it has often been suggested that there is an inevitable tendency for improvements (in child-rearing as in other fields) to be adopted sooner by those higher in the social scale, and only to be taken up by those at the bottom after a considerable lapse of time. To the extent that this is valid, it would imply that, even when the grosser forms of poverty have been finally eliminated, 'cultural lag' will still operate to preserve the differences in the mortality risks to which infants in the different social classes are exposed. There is obviously some truth in this. Professor Illsley of Aberdeen, for example, has shown how the various social classes approach courtship, marriage, home-making and parenthood with widely' different maturity, experience and preparation. 'When they reach the stage of motherhood, the various social groups must differ widely in physical and emotional maturity, and this must condition their performance both in the clinical course of pregnancy and labour and in the wider sphere of motherhood and the rearing of a family.' As he points out, 'it seem inevitable that the lower class girl should lean more heavily on traditional methods of child care'.

In this sense the differences seem likely to persist. The National Birthday Trust survey showed that the influence of social class was still important in England and Wales as recently as 1958 in perinatal deaths (still births and the loss of infant life during birth and the first seven days). And official figures for Scotland (where the gradient has always been very similar to the England and Wales one) suggest that 1961 still showed the same social class differential in infant mortality. However, the most recent investigation in England and Wales seems to foreshadow a break in this long-standing social class gradient. Dr Spicer and Dr Lipworth extracted registration data relating to infant deaths occurring between 1 April 1964 and 31 March 1965. For the 'populations at risk' to relate to these infant deaths in their various groupings they used a 10 per cent sample of births registered from 1 July 1963 to 30 June 1964. Although the numbers in their statistical cells made it necessary for them to amalgamate the Registrar General's first two Social Class Groups and also to do the same for the last two (leaving only three separate groups in all), the social class gradient certainly looks less steep even when allowance is made for the effects of these amalgamations. Thus for England and Wales as a whole, neonatal deaths per thousand live births were 9·2 for Social Classes I and II combined, 11·8 for Class III, and 13·2 for Classes IV and V combined. The corresponding postneonatal death rates for these three Social Class Groups were 3·5, 5·4, and 7·6 respectively. These figures have, however, to be looked at in the light of the marked regional differences found to exist, which could not be explained as due to the effects of either social class or the mother's age or parity (i.e. whether it was her first, second or *nth* child). Babies born in the southern and eastern parts of England were at a substantial advantage by comparison with those born in Wales and the North of England. When the social class differences within each of the regions are examined, some very interesting results emerge. The North of England showed, for both neonatal and post-neonatal mortality, a social class gradient of the traditional type, with statistically significant differences between each of the social class groups. All other regions showed a break in the gradient in one or other of the series, in that at some point no statistically significant difference emerged; in some cases only the combined Group IV and V was significantly different from the rest, in others only the combined Group I and II. In areas of England and Wales other than the North it certainly looks as though the effects of poverty and the 'cultural lag' in maintaining class differentials in infant mortality have been, for the first time, seriously weakened.

General mortality by social class

The process of 'marrying' census material with death registration data has also been undertaken by the Registrar General for England and Wales for some time past in respect of general mortality. In order to do this, standard mortality ratios have been calculated for occupied and retired men in each of the five Social Class Groups. These standard mortality ratios are the ratios of *actual* numbers of deaths to the numbers that would have been *expected* if the overall national mortality rates at different ages were applied to the population within each social class. Where the ratio is 100, the mortality experience of that social class exactly corresponds to the experience of the population as a whole at that date; where the ratio is less than 100 the mortality experience is more favourable and where it is more than 100 the mortality experience is less favourable. On this basis, standard mortality ratios for occupied and retired men showed, around the time of the 1921 Census, a social class gradient, with ratios of 82 for Social Class I, and ratios of 94, 95, 101 and 125 for the remaining Social Class Groups in that order.

When similar figures were prepared around the time of the 1931 Census there was still seen to be a gradient, but it was appreciably less steep at the extremes. The corresponding ratios on that occasion started with 90 for Social Class I and continued with ratios of 94, 97, 102 and 111 in that order. When preliminary figures of the same type were produced around the time of the 1951 Census they appeared to represent a major and highly favourable change in the situation as compared with the prewar period. The provisional ratios were 97 for Social Class I, followed by 86, 102, 94 and 118 in that order. No wonder this was felt by the *Manchester Guardian* to be front page news to be presented to its readers under the title 'Mortality Amended'. For the first time in the history of this country it seemed as though a man's expectation of life was no longer inseparably linked with his social position. Those in Social Class II appeared to have a more favourable mortality experience than their fellows in higher status occupations, and the semiskilled manual workers of Social Class IV also appeared to be more favourably situated in mortality terms than those in the top Social Class Group (not to mention those in the Class immediately above them). The so-called W-effect represented by this startling series of figures was widely discussed. And though the Registrar General reminded his readers that the findings of one year were not conclusive and that the full 1951 Census tabulations were not yet available, it was natural that explanations of the new situation should abound. Not expectedly, in these 'lay' explanations two features tended to predominate. First, there was great emphasis on the special risks to which those in posts of high responsibility in business and elsewhere were supposed to be peculiarly prone, and much was made of ulcers and heart disease. Secondly, the apparently highly favourable situation of semi-skilled manual workers was held to demonstrate the benefits already accruing from postwar improvements in standards of life and social and health facilities, notably the infant National Health Service.

Rejoicing over the apparent replacement of the social class gradient in general mortality by the W-effect proved, however, to have been premature. For in course of time, when fuller information became available and a closer look had been taken at the position both by those in the General Register Office and outside it, several potentially misleading aspects of these 1950 ratios came to light. First, changes in the allocation of occupations to Social Classes between the 1931 and the 1951 Census shifted over half a million men *out* of Social Class IV and an even larger number *into* it; and it so happened that the occupations involved in this transfer differed in their mortality experience. By putting these occupations back in their 1931 Social Classes, the 1950 standard mortality·ratio for men aged 20–64 in Social Class IV is brought up from the low figure of 94 which had caused such astonishment to 104, which re-establishes the social class gradient in the lower half of the social heirarchy. This left only Social Class I remaining out of its traditional relationship with the other four. A possible, indeed highly probable contributory factor here, was the different way in which the category of company directors was treated for census purposes and at death registration respectively. For census purposes only directors of *more than* one company were classified as company directors. At death registration, however, no similar limitation of this category seems to have been applied, making it highly probable that a high proportion of those so classified at death would, on census criteria, have figured as managers and appeared in Social Class II. When Professors Illsley and Allcorn tried moving *all* company directors out of Social Class I (where they only formed less than one-half of 1 per cent of the population) to Social Class II, and recalculated the 1950 standard mortality ratios after this adjustment, the revised ratios proved to be the same for both these social classes (88) in the case of men aged 20–64. When they made a similar calculation after transferring all company directors' *wives* from I to II, the married women's ratios became 86 for Social Class I and 90 for Social Class II, instead of 96 and 88 respectively as they had been before this transfer was made. If one accepts the view that, in all the circumstances, the fairest thing to do *is* to move all those coded as company directors (or their wives) into the lower status category, then the social class gradient has triumphantly reasserted itself.

Until the occupational populations of the 1961 Census have been 'married' with the mortality information of similar date, we shall not know whether general mortality still, in the 1960s, increases with depressing regularity as one descends the social scale. As it is not officially expected that the first volumes of the Registrar General's *Decennial Supplement for 1961* will be published until the middle or end of 1967, the reader will have to look for the relevant standard mortality ratios when they appear. No one seriously doubts that, in the end, the gradient will disappear. Already there are highly favourable results to report amongst children; at ages 1–2 years, for example, the gap in mortality between Social Class I and Social Class V is only a fraction of what it was as recently as twenty years ago. It can only be a matter of time before the gap is closed equally successfully for other age groups as well.

Social class gradient in fertility

It had always been realised that the tendency towards voluntary family limitation in Britain began in the upper social strata and spread to working class families only gradually. Thanks to the Family Census of 1946, conducted by Professors Glass and Grebenik for the Royal Commission on Population, we know a great deal more about the changing family-building patterns in the different social strata than we did before this special census was undertaken. There had been no fertility census in Britain since 1911, and only since 1938 had such vital information as the age of the mother been recorded at the time of registering a birth. A 10 per cent random sample (made possible by the ration book exchange of 1945) was taken of women who at that time were married or had been married. Each woman in the sample was asked in January/February 1946 to supply the dates of her birth, of her first marriage (and, if ended, of its termination), and of the births of every live-born child she had had. She was also asked for information about her husband's occupation. The whole enquiry was on an entirely voluntary basis, but the high proportion of 87 per cent of the sample cooperated by furnishing the required information. Table 5 compares the experience of those married early in the present century, with the most recent marriage cohort in the sample whose child-bearing was virtually complete. It can be seen that the overall mean number of births per woman had declined from 3·53 to 2·42 in twenty years or so. But there was also a social class gradient for the marriages of the later as well as those of the earlier period, when the women were grouped according to their

TABLE 5

Former family size in the different social strata in Great Britain (all marriages under 45 years of age)

Occupational category of husband		Number of live births per woman first married in	
		1900–09	1920–24
Non-manual	Professional	2·33	1·75
Group	Employers	2·64	1·84
	Own account	2·96	1·95
	Farmers and farm managers	3·50	2·31
	Salaried employees	2·37	1·65
	Non-manual wage earners	2·89	1·97
Manual	Manual wage earners	3·96	2·70
Group	Agricultural workers	3·88	2·71
	Labourers	4·45	3·35
All Categories		3·53	2·42

Source. D. V. Glass and E. Grebenik, *The Trend and Pattern of Fertility in Great Britain* (Family Census 1946) (Royal Commission on Population).

husbands' occupations. The mean number of children born to the wives of manual wage-earners was considerably higher, in each period, than the number born to the wives of men in the professions. The same was also true within the agricultural sphere, where the wives of farmers and farm managers had smaller families than those of agricultural workers. Two points are worth particular notice. First, the social class differential in fertility was, looked at in one way, no more important than the steady decline in family size that had been taking place. Thus the wives of manual workers married between 1920 and 1924 had families of much the same size as those of employers in the 1900–1909 groups; and going back in time even further, average numbers of children amongst the wives of unskilled labourers married between 1900 and 1909 were only slightly higher than those of employers married between 1890 and 1899. Secondly, the least fertile group was, in 1920–24, not that in the *highest* status category, but the one a little way down the status scale; the social class gradient had a V-effect, in that families were larger both above and below the group of wives of salaried employees. A newspaper headline of the time aptly summarised the position—'The Unproductive Clerk'.

An interesting example of the social class gradient in fertility is provided by the case of the teaching profession. A large national sample of women who entered teaching at various dates prewar and postwar after teacher-training of different types was recently followed up and asked for dates and details of family-building and careers. Those who entered teaching in 1936 had, by 1960, completed their family-building. Of two of the types of teacher involved (graduates with a teacher-training and two-year trained non-graduates) it was the non-graduates who had the lower mean number of live-born children per first marriage, 1·63; the graduates, though they tended to marry somewhat later in life, had a larger number, 1·71. These figures from my study *Women and Teaching*, correspond fairly closely to those relating to the wives of men teachers in Mrs Jean Floud's national sample of teachers teaching in 1955; for when that material was analysed, Dr Wolf Scott found that, for marriages before 1945, and taking the first ten years of marriage, the mean size of the grammar school teacher's family was 0·09 children *larger* than that of the non-grammar school teacher. The figures are also very much in line with the Family Census data already discussed. Thus the non-graduate women teachers had families very similar in size to those of the wives of 'salaried employees', where the mean number of live births per woman first married in 1920–24 was, as we have seen, 1·65; while the university graduates amongst the women who entered teaching corresponded fairly closely with the Family Census 'professional' category, where the women first married in 1920–24 who had husbands in that occupational group had a mean number of live births of 1·75.

Do the latest available figures confirm the persistence of the social class differentials amongst the Family Census women married in 1920–24? There are two difficulties in giving a satisfactory answer to this question. One arises from the fact that the appropriate 1961 Census fertility data are given in terms of the Registrar General's sixteen Socio-Economic Groups, which are not always easy to 'match' with the occupational categories used in the Family Census. The second difficulty is that, in the relevant tables of the 1961 Census, mean family size is given for a wide variety of ages at marriage and durations of marriage, and the social class differentials are not by any means uniform for the wide variety of groups that can be separately distinguished in this way. If, for example, we take those whose age at marriage was 20–24, and look first at family size for all durations of marriage, we find mean family sizes for the wives of manual workers ranging from 2·55 (for the unskilled) through 2·16 (for the semi-skilled) to 1·92 (the skilled). The wives of self-employed professional workers (2·10) have larger families than those of employers and managers (1·81 and 1·83 for those in large and small establishments respectively); while the nearest categories to the 'salaried employees' have almost the lowest mean number of children (intermediate non-manual workers, 1·64; junior non-manual workers 1·67), except for professional workers who are employees (1·58). There is some evidence here of a social class gradient of the traditional pattern, but the 'all durations of marriage' group must include substantial numbers of women who were married a long time ago.

Taking the same age at marriage (20–24), but confining our attention to marriages which had only lasted five years at the time of the 1961 Census, the mean family sizes for unskilled, semi-skilled and skilled manual workers still follow the expected pattern (1·74, 1·47, 1·36). The wives of self-employed professional workers (1·69) are still tending to have more children than those in the skilled manual group, but this time also more than those in the semi-skilled manual group; and, as before, more than the two groups of employers and managers (1·32, 1·37). The intermediate and junior non-manual workers groups have the lowest numbers of children (1·29, 1·20) but are this time bracketed with the wives of manual-working foremen and supervisors (1·27) who had previously been *higher* than the skilled manual group rather than lower; while the wives of professional workers who are employees have ceased to be the least fertile group of all, and reached instead much the same position as the employers and managers groups *and* the skilled manual group. Despite these rather confusing differences, it looks as though, if five-years marriage duration is long enough to judge by, a broadly similar pattern of social class differentials to the traditional one is to be found in family-building amongst those married at 20–24 and still relatively young at the time of the 1961 Census.

Clearly all the demographic trends indicated in earlier chapters have social implications, farreaching or otherwise. All that can be done in the present chapter is to pick out a few examples and comment briefly upon them.

The role of the middle-aged married woman

The tendency to marry younger, the broad trend towards smaller families, and the increased expectation of life, have between them meant that today's married woman is free of family-building and family-rearing responsibilities much earlier than her grandmother was, and that she can expect to live to an older age. She therefore has a very substantially longer span of years in which, in theory at least, she can do other things. If we take, for example, the middle-class married woman, other developments have reinforced the purely demographic ones in this respect. Labour-saving domestic arrangements have replaced the housework nightmare of the Victorian home. Looking after one's elderly parents tends to take less onerous forms than used to be the case, and children leave home earlier. The home itself has become less important as a centre of social activities; and so on. Although the greatly extended span of years theoretically available to engage in other activities has been partly matched by extended opportunities for middle-class married women to engage in paid employment, part-time and full-time, outside the home, it is generally agreed that reliance on increased economic activity rates in the middle age groups will not be enough. Nor have voluntary organisations so far succeeded in filling the gap. Both from their own and from society's point of view we clearly cannot afford to be complacent about a situation in which important sections of our population in the prime of life are left in the unhappy position of having fulfilled the main part of their role long before their capacity to play a full part in the community's life has been exhausted.

The disappearing spinster

It is obvious to anyone that the elimination of the earlier preponderance of women in the marriageable age groups and the greatly increased marriage intensity of recent years, carry the implication that unmarried women over 20 are likely to be very few in number in the future. This, in its turn, means that professions such as teaching and nursing, where single women used to form the major constituent, will increasingly have either to depend on men or to adapt themselves to the needs of married women. This may, of course, take the form of a two-part career, in which young women train for one of these professions as at present and then, after a brief spell of service (or none at all) concentrate on family-building and rearing and have a phased return to the work for which they are trained later (if indeed they ever return). Or it may mean that training is itself split into two parts, one to be undertaken before marriage and the other only when a worthwhile period of full-time service is contemplated. Or the whole training may be postponed until the women concerned are in their late twenties or early thirties. Whichever plan is ultimately adopted, the whole development clearly has far-reaching implications for professions of these types. The virtual disappearance of the spinster must inevitably have even wider repercussions on many other aspects of British life, and furnishes yet another example of the wide-ranging effects that demographic trends can have.

An ageing population

It is clear that, by comparison with the prewar position, our population is an ageing one; and though the proportion of people aged 65 and over may be very slightly less by the end of this century than it is at present (see Table 6), their absolute numbers are likely to have increased by over $1\frac{1}{2}$ million. The possible social implications of this are farreaching. The so-called 'burden of dependency', comparing the relative numbers of those under and over working age with those of working age, will almost certainly be much heavier by the end of the century, and is already substantially greater than it was thirty or forty years ago. Some economists have suggested that it is not so much that providing for this dependent population will *directly* put an undue strain on our economic resources, but rather that the

TABLE 6

Age and sex structure of the estimated mid-1966 England and Wales total population compared with (a) the 1931 Census and (b) the official projection of the estimated mid-1965 total population to 2001 (Figures in thousands)

	1931		1966		2001	
	Number	%	Number	%	Number	%
Under 15						
Males	4,808		5,668		9,591	
Females	4,712		5,389		9,075	
Total	9,520	23·8	11,057	22·9	18,666	28·1
15–64						
Males	13,053		15,591		20,398	
Females	14,416		15,619		19,789	
Total	27,469	68·8	31,210	64·8	40,187	60·5
65 and over						
Males	1,272		2,245		3,144	
Females	1,691		3,677		4,426	
Total	2,963	7·4	5,922	12·3	7,570	11·4
All ages						
Males	19,133		23,504		33,133	
Females	20,819		24,685		33,290	
Total	39,952	100·0	48,189	100·0	66,423	100·0

Sources. Registrar General for England and Wales, Quarterly Returns for 4th quarter of 1965 and 3rd quarter of 1966; Census, 1931.
Note. Assumptions underlying the projection are discussed in Chapter 10.

necessary taxing of the economically productive section of the community to transfer resources on this scale to the non-producers may seriously reduce the incentives on which our economic well-being and progress depend. Such a budgetary or transfer problem could, of course, be accentuated if the potential voting power of those over working age were ever used to raise pensions to a level likely to cripple the economy either directly or indirectly. This possibility was very much in the mind of the late Lord Beveridge when preparing his report *Social Insurance and Allied Services* (1942), and had much to do with his insistence that pensions under the state scheme should be tied to a level at, but not above, subsistence. Up till now, of course, those over pensionable age have not been organised into a pressure group powerful enough to secure what most of us would regard as reasonable state benefits, let alone unreasonably high ones.

Quite apart from the possible budgetary implications of the increasing numbers over pensionable age, there are many other issues raised, or greatly accentuated, by this development. Take, for instance, the question of old people living alone. Every social worker is aware that far too many elderly people are isolated from their families and their fellow citizens, that their lives are too often characterised by quite inadequate diets, medical provision, heating and domestic comfort and social contact. Facts and figures are not always available to show the magnitude of this problem, but it comes as a shock to learn from the 1961 Census that there are in England and Wales no fewer than 1,084,000 people over pensionable age living alone (that is, forming one-person households). As would be expected from the sex differential in life expectancy *and* from the lower pensionable age for women, some 921,000 of these are women. The proportion this particular type of one-person household forms of all households is nearly $7\frac{1}{2}$ per cent, which by any standard seems far too high.

The increasing number of old people tends to make even more pressing the need to re-examine the whole question of compulsory or normal retirement. Now that the average span of useful life has been greatly extended, ought the conventional retirement ages decided on many years ago to be extended also? Ideally, everyone ought to be able to go on working, full-time or part-time, as long as he wants to, provided he is fit enough and provided he is not being driven to do so by economic necessity. It is believed that about a third of the male population over 65 would like to be gainfully employed for at least part of the working week; but present state pension arrangements tend to face them with an 'all or nothing' choice, in which they either have to remain in full-time employment (and earn increments to the pension eventually drawn for each year beyond 65), or virtually give up paid employment altogether except for a few hours work a week. Yet *raising* the pensionable age (though suggested some years ago by members of a Committee on the Economic and Financial Problems of Provision for Old Age) seems to the public mind too like putting the clock back: earlier retirement, like shorter hours, has been for so long an objective of social policy to which everyone at least paid lip-service. Flexibility in our arrangements, so as to make it possible for the individual to remain in paid employment of some kind (with appropriate safeguards for the younger men waiting to step into his shoes) to exactly the extent that suits his own particular needs and preferences, is eminently desirable but extremely difficult to achieve in practice.

In many ways more fundamental than any of the other aspects of an ageing population is the change that has come about in the position of old people as a result of rapid and revolutionary changes in knowledge, particularly in the technological and scientific fields. It used to be some compensation to the old for the weakening of their physical and mental powers that they were at least valued by the younger generation as sources of accumulated knowledge, wisdom and experience. Inevitably today much of this 'capital of experience' is no longer relevant and has become out of date. To the extent that this has happened, the whole status of the older members of our society has suffered a serious blow: the impairment of their usefulness in transmitting the fruits of their experience to others tends, if we put it in an extreme form, to make them objects of pity or even ridicule rather than veneration. This is, of course, an exaggerated picture. It is, in any case, much less true of women than it is of men. The work of Professor Townsend and others has shown how much, in the areas they have studied, married daughters rely on the advice and guidance of their mothers. Indeed, where kinship ties of this type have been broken as a result of rehousing younger families in new districts far removed from the older generation, great hardship to both has often resulted. The old are still needed by the young; but there has, nevertheless, been a significant change of emphasis highly damaging to the self-esteem of the old, and modifying their role in society. Much more thought will have to be given to the part that they can still usefully play, and in helping them to play that part.

The social implications of an ageing population are, then, both farreaching and fundamental. We cannot alter the basic facts of the situation; but we can, and must, make the necessary changes in our family and social policy to enable as many as possible of our older citizens to make a constructive contribution to our social life, both in our interests and in theirs. Much has already been heard, and more is bound to be heard in the future, about, for example, the loneliness of old age. Though not an entirely new problem, both its nature and its scale have changed. In the days when few survived to their sixties, and when those tough enough to do so had a positive and valued role in the circle of the extended family, there was much less scope for loneliness. Preparation for retirement is another obvious example. Everyone today agrees that more and more encouragement and help must be given to ease the transition to retirement, and to enable people to prepare themselves for the entirely new situation with which they are likely to be faced. Such a need hardly existed in the days when you either died by middle age or went on working virtually to the end of your useful life.

Housing and household sizes

Housing represents one of the most obvious types of case in which population census data can form a factual basis for social policy. For not only is a good deal of information about the houses in which people live collected at census time, but the characteristics (in terms of both size and structure) of the households at present occupying these houses, are also recorded. As a natural and necessary accompaniment of the particular type of population increase we have experienced over the last half century, the number of *households* has hitherto grown much more than the number of *people*. In Great Britain between 1911 and 1961 households increased by about 80 per cent while the population only rose by 26 per cent or so. Between the same dates the mean size of households declined from 4·5 persons to 3·1 persons. Where the number of children per completed family has been falling, this is what one would expect. Yet long after these developments had shown themselves to be part of our population growth pattern, the standard three-bedroom house continued to predominate in new building; both private and local authority building programmes were at the same time insufficient in amount and unsuitable in unit size for the needs that should have been obvious. It is certainly to be hoped that, in formulating future housing policy, much more account will be taken of the mass of demographic material now available bearing on both present and projected future numbers and sizes of households in each local authority area. In terms purely of numbers of *people*, current projections (discussed in a later chapter) imply the need to provide, in England and Wales, housing for a *new* population the size of a city such as Sheffield every year for the next thirty-five years.

Emigration

Figures showing the annual number of emigrants, though important, only tell part of the story. To assess the effect of any given rate of emigration we need to know for how long the emigrants will be away; on what scale they will send back remittances to the home country; whether they will come back to retire, and if so whether they will bring their life savings with them. These and other obvious considerations are important, and we can often only attach figures to them by looking at the behaviour of emigrants' predecessors. But it is the *selective* effects of emigration that have caused most concern in Britain in recent years. For emigrants from this country are clearly not a random sample of the population. There used to be more men than women among them, though this is no longer so today. They tend to be younger than the average of the home population. It is usual to suggest that they are also more virile and more enterprising —in fact, just the kind of people no country can afford to lose. Indeed, if a balance-sheet type of approach is adopted, the loss of a direct return for society's investment in their education and up-bringing is often quoted; just at the time when they cease to be purely consumers and are ready to make their contribution as pro-ducers, some other country reaps the reward. And the more highly qualified and highly educated they are, the more popular alarm and indignation tends to be aroused by their departure. The wide accept-ance of the term 'brain drain' implies a one-way outward movement of a highly selective character on a scale with disastrous implications even in the short-term. The 'fact' of the so-called 'brain drain' can, moreover, be used to support arguments of a widely differing and even contradictory nature. Governments are not spending enough on scientific research and development; the salaries and working con-ditions of scientists in public employ compare so unfavourably with opportunities elsewhere that they emigrate. Alternatively, Govern-ments are spending too much; and the crippling level of direct taxes to which our scientists, whether in public or private employ, are subject, drives them to leave this country.

We have already seen, in Chapter 6, that reliable official figures enabling us to be sure what is the present annual net loss in any given category of skill, are not yet available, though an early improve-ment in the statistics of emigration is promised. In view of our lack of suitable data, neither the true extent nor the possible implications of the 'brain drain' can at present be determined. Even in a case where we are told officially what the current net loss amounts to, as in the case of qualified medical practitioners, the loss can be made to seem relatively unimportant or to seem alarming by setting it against different background features, as has already been shown. It is, of course, known that American agencies have for some time been making strenuous efforts to recruit talent of many kinds in Britain. This may, as Mr Quintin Hogg suggested in a recent debate, amount to 'plundering the educational systems of Western Europe', but present Government policy does not contemplate any attempt to prevent action of this kind, in the belief that prohibition will not prove effective.

Immigration

If the image of a 'brain drain' has recently given emigration a highly unfavourable connotation in the British public's mind, the rapidly growing immigration of the years up to mid-1962 created an equally unfortunate public impression. For despite the fact that those at least whose schooling had taken place in Britain had been taught what great benefits, material and other, had accrued to this country from *earlier* waves of immigrants, there seemed to be many features of the situation in the late 1950s and early 1960s that were different from previous occasions. For one thing, these were not to any marked degree refugees from political, racial or religious persecution. Nor were they from Europe. They came in larger numbers, from different areas and for different reasons from their predecessors. And though they provided a much needed addition to our overstretched labour force (and in nursing, in particular, the public gratitude for their help was both genuine and general), their coming came to be associated in the public mind with race riots in Nottingham and Notting Hill—a new and ugly feature of contemporary British life— and there were dark forebodings of what might happen when employment was no longer so full, when overcrowding and health problems became more acute as the flow continued. It was widely believed that assimilation was proving difficult if not impossible in many cases; and that the economic and other difficulties faced by the immigrants were leading them to settle in certain parts of the cities to which they went, with the consequent emergence for the first time of 'coloured quarters' with their attendant social evils and dangers.

As with the emigration case, there was a crying need for authoritative facts and figures, and amongst those who undertook special surveys to fill this need was Mrs Ruth Glass. In her study, *New-comers*, she obtained information about a large sample of West Indians who had settled in London, between the beginning of 1954 and the end of 1958. Careful analysis of this material, together with published statistics from a wide variety of sources, enabled her to dispel a number of myths. She demonstrated, for example, that the widely held belief that almost all the newcomers were unskilled workers before they came here was unjustified. One in four of the men had, in fact, been non-manual workers, and only one in five had been semi-skilled or unskilled workers or farm labourers. The migrants' job aspirations on arrival here had, of course, often not been fulfilled; downgrading, in status if not in economic terms, had been a common experience. The mistaken belief that almost all Commonwealth immigrants were completely unskilled gained some support even from official pronouncements of the time, despite the cautious wording used. In the Second Report of the Oversea Migration Board in 1956, for example, this sentence occurs. 'We are doubtful whether those who are now increasing the figures of immigrants into this country are as skilled in trades and professions as those who are emigrating to other parts of the Commonwealth, and whether they can be assimilated without some difficulties into the economic and social life of this country.'

A debate in the House of Lords on 3 November 1966 showed what widely differing views on most aspects of the immigration problem were held even amongst relatively well-informed people. Amongst the many questions that this debate, like so many others, left unresolved, were some of a highly practical character. First, do British Governments need greater powers to control immigration from the Commonwealth than they had before 1 July 1962? If the answer is 'yes', was the *form* of the control provided by the Commonwealth Immigrants Act of 1962 the appropriate one? If the answer is again 'yes', has the use made of these controls since then been wise or foolish; should our policy have been more liberal or more stringent? In that debate Lord Stonham, speaking for the Government, said that their policy was to control the immigration of permanent residents at a level related to the economic need of the country and its capacity to absorb the newcomers into the community, while rejecting any vestige of discrimination on the grounds of race, colour, or religion. It was also Government policy to treat the family as a natural unit, and so long as voucher holders were admitted their dependants would also be admitted. He gave figures to show that over the previous three years admissions against vouchers had steadily declined. In 1964 there were 14,705 admissions; in 1965 12,880; and in 1966 (the complete figure for which has only become available since he made his speech) 5,461. The 1966 admissions were therefore only about a third of those in 1964 and half of those in 1965. It is clearly impossible for the ordinary citizen, who does not know the evidence on which the economic needs of the country and its capacity to absorb further Commonwealth immigrants are based, to form a reasoned opinion as to whether this much reduced number of Ministry of Labour vouchers issued is too small or still too large. As a footnote to all this it may be noted that some 42,000 dependants accompanying or coming to join the head of the household were also admitted to the United Kingdom in 1966; in addition, Commonwealth citizens who came as visitors for three months or less numbered 222,500 or so, there were 21,500 visitors for longer periods, and about 14,000 students were admitted under the provisions of the Act.

National population projections

There is an obvious need, particularly amongst those concerned with future planning in many different fields, to have some idea of the likely future size and age and sex structure of our population. To meet this need, it would be possible to produce a variety of projections based on alternative assumptions; to show, as it were, the results likely to come about by taking extremely optimistic assumptions and extremely pessimistic ones, and to leave the planner to choose where, between these extremes, he thought the appropriate expectation for his purposes might lie. Rather than publish sets of alternative official projections of this kind, however, the present policy in this country is to publish annually *one* official projection, and to modify this in subsequent years as seems appropriate. In any one year there is therefore only one official projection for general use, so that possible confusion in the public mind arising from the publication of alternative projections is avoided. For this purpose the Registrars General of England and Wales, Scotland and Northern Ireland, and the Government Actuary, agree on the assumptions they propose to make that year, and the resulting projections are published separately for the constituent countries and for the U.K. as a whole.

If we take the official projection of the estimated mid-1965 total population of England and Wales as our example, the assumptions underlying this projection fall into the usual three groups of mortality, natality and migration. The mortality assumptions are not difficult to agree upon. At ages *under* 40, death rates are assumed to decline steadily over the period of the projection until, by the year 2001, they are only half or less of the current rates. At ages *over* 40 the assumed rates of decline become progressively smaller with

D

advancing age and vanish at ages over 90. The natality assumptions are that yearly live births will be 869,000 in 1965–66 and will gradually increase thereafter to 948,000 in 1970, 1,008,000 in 1980, 1,199,000 in 1990 and 1,364,000 in 2000. It is also assumed that the ratio of male to female live births remains at the present figure of 1·06 throughout the period. Ever since the mid-1950s, when the number of births recorded each year began, for the first time since the 'bulge' years of 1946 and 1947, to show an increase every time over the previous year, some account has had to be taken of this in making these projections. At first, caution had to be exercised, as the 'boom in babies' might have been only a temporary phenomenon; but as it became clear that this was no mere passing phase, the natality assumptions were modified in an upward direction for each new projection. Largely as a result of changing assumptions about natality, the official population projection for England and Wales around the last years of the twentieth and the first years of the twenty-first century increased by some twenty million in the nine years from 1955 to 1964 (or slightly less than this if allowance is made for the fact that the 1964 projection was to the year 2001, whereas the 1955 one was only to 1995). If the downturn in recorded births which began in 1965 should, in its turn, prove to be more than a temporary phenomenon, the natality assumptions on which the projections of the *next* few years are based will have to be correspondingly scaled down, with similar results in modifying the projected population at the turn of the century, though this time in the opposite direction.

In the current projection of the estimated mid-1965 total England and Wales population, the assumptions relating to migration take the following form. It is assumed that a net inward migration from all sources of the order of 53,000 will take place in 1965–66, declining to 35,000 in 1970–71 and 18,000 in 1978–79 and subsequently. It is also assumed that this net migration will be $47\frac{1}{2}$ per cent male and $52\frac{1}{2}$ per cent female, this in order to reflect the expected increase in the importance of dependants of previous immigrants in future immigration. It is of interest to see what the constituent elements in these assumed migration figures are. The assumed net inward movement of 53,000 in 1965–66 is made up of a net outward movement of

96,000 U.K. passport holders going beyond the British Isles, a net *inward* movement of similar dimensions (95,000) on non-U.K. passports, a net inward traffic from Eire of 30,000, and a net inward flow from Scotland and Northern Ireland together of 24,000. The assumed reduction to a net inward movement into England and Wales of 35,000 in 1970–71 is mainly brought about by assuming a fall of 10,000 in the net inward movement to England and Wales from Scotland and Northern Ireland, this being reinforced by assuming a 7,000 larger net outward movement of U.K. passport holders to countries beyond the British Isles. The subsequent decline in the assumed net inward movement into England and Wales to only 18,000 in 1978–79 and subsequent years arises from assuming a still further fall (to only 7,000) in the net inward movement from Scotland and Northern Ireland, and a 10,000 reduction in the net inward movement to England and Wales of those with Commonwealth passports; other net movements are assumed to continue at roughly their previous levels.

The progressive reductions assumed in the net population intake to England and Wales from Scotland and Northern Ireland is, in fact, entirely concentrated on Scotland, and clearly implies the expectation that the economic rehabilitation and strengthening of that country will progressively curtail the outward drift of population which has been experienced in the past; the net movement from Scotland to England and Wales is taken as being roughly halved each five years during the next fifteen years. Northern Ireland is assumed to be going to continue to have a net loss of population to England and Wales of 4,000 a year (and, incidentally, to Scotland of 1,000 and to the rest of the world of 3,000). Scotland's assumed net outward migration balance with countries *outside* the United Kingdom of 16,000 in 1965–66 is expected to fall to 10,000 by 1967–68 and to 8,000 a year in 1974–75 and subsequent years. Here, too, it is clearly anticipated that a better economic balance as between Scotland on the one hand and England and Wales on the other will reduce emigration overseas from Scotland. The present size of this is indicated by the 1964 estimate of some 22,000 U.K. passport holders leaving Scotland for destinations beyond the United Kingdom as intending emigrants; the corresponding figure for England was

169,000 whereas, if such overseas movement had been on a scale proportionate to the Scottish one, it would have been 186,000.

Adding together the assumed population movements affecting the constituent countries, the assumed migration balance for the United Kingdom as a whole becomes a net annual immigration of 10,000 until 1971, dwindling to nil in 1975–76 and thereafter. The main elements in this, as will have been gathered from the previous discussion, are an indefinite continuance of net immigration from Eire at the 30,000 a year rate, and from foreign countries also at 30,000 a year; net immigration from Commonwealth countries is assumed to be at the rate of 70,000 a year to begin with, falling from 1975 onwards to 60,000 (this being responsible for the overall United Kingdom position changing from plus 10,000 to nil). The net outflow of United Kingdom citizens is assumed to continue indefinitely at the 120,000 a year level.

Three points should be noted about these migration assumptions. In the first place, the actual movements of recent years (particularly the overseas ones) may be a very poor guide to what is likely to happen ten, twenty or thirty years hence. There is, therefore, a very real sense in which more guesswork is involved in making migration assumptions than in making assumptions about natality and mortality. Secondly, the figures of net migration balance either way incorporated in the current official projection for the United Kingdom are small, both in relation to the size of our population and in relation to the natural increase of that population by excess of births over deaths. Thirdly, some account has been taken, in the projection, of the greater fertility of Commonwealth immigrants in recent years compared with the home population.

The combined result of applying the assumptions described above in respect of mortality, natality and migration to the estimated mid-1965 total population of England and Wales is to produce a projected population for the year 2001 of nearly $66\frac{1}{2}$ million. For comparison with the past position there are obvious advantages in choosing 1931, a census year; and 1966 comes exactly midway between this and the year 2001, the latest year for which current official projections are made. By using 1966 as an indication of the present position, therefore, the experience of the thirty-five-year period 1931–66 can be contrasted with current official expectations for the *next* thirty-five years, 1966–2001. Comparing the current projected total population in 2001 (based on the estimated *mid-1965* total population) of nearly 66½ million with the estimated mid-1966 total population of nearly 48¼ million, the present official expectation is, then, of an increase of the order of 18,234,000 or 37·8 per cent in the next thirty-five years, an average annual increase of some 521,000. In the thirty-five years *before* 1966 the population of England and Wales increased by about 8,237,000 or 20·6 per cent, an average annual increase of some 235,000. It is therefore clear that the average yearly increase of the England and Wales population officially expected in the next thirty-five years is more than twice as great as was in fact experienced in the *last* thirty-five years.

The interest and importance of population projections is not, of course, limited to the extent and rate of overall change in numbers. It is also of considerable interest to know how the sex ratio in the various age groups is likely to change, and how the proportions between the age groups are likely to alter. Taking the sex ratio first, and again using as our example the England and Wales position, the number of males per 1,000 females in the under 15 age group rose from 1,020 in 1931 to 1,051 in 1965. On the current official projection this figure would increase to 1,057 by the year 2001. Similarly, in the 15 to 64 age group there used, in 1931, to be 905 men for every 1,000 women. By 1965 this figure had increased to 997, and the current projection implies 1,031 men for every 1,000 women. The tendency for the proportion of men to women to increase carries through to the 65 and over age group. In 1931 there were only 752 men per 1,000 women in this group. By 1965 the figures had fallen to 608 but, by the year 2001, it is expected to rise again, though only to 710. Grandmothers will continue to exceed grandfathers in number, but not to quite the extent that they do at present. The disparity between the sexes gets greater very rapidly as the higher ages are reached. Thus in the 65–69 age group there are likely to be, by the year 2001, 893 men for every 1,000 women. But amongst those of 85 and over there will only be 370. It should be remembered, of course, that these projected changes in the ratio between the sexes are all arrived at on the assumption that the present proportions between live-born boys and live-born girls continue to operate.

We are all familiar with the way in which natality changes work their way through a population, for we have watched the babies of the 'bulge' years affect the number of schoolchildren in the different age groups for whom our education authorities have had to provide. This happens to be a rather spectacular instance, but changes both in fertility and in mortality are constantly working their way through any population in similar fashion. Inevitably, therefore, both the absolute numbers and the proportions in the various age groups have changed and will continue to change. Comparing the estimated mid-1966 total population of England and Wales with the 1931 Census, the number of children under 15 has risen by over $1\frac{1}{2}$ million, but they still form roughly the same proportion (22·9 per cent as against 23·8 per cent) of the total. The official expectation is that, by the end of the century, there will be over $7\frac{1}{2}$ million more children in this age group, and that they will then form a higher proportion (28·1 per cent) of the total. Numbers in the 15–64 group have risen by some 3,700,000 in the last thirty-five years, and are expected to increase by a further 9,100,000 by the turn of the century. By that date, however, they may only form some 60·5 per cent of the whole population as against the present figure of 64·8 per cent and the proportion thirty-five years ago of 68·8 per cent. Those of 65 and over have already increased by nearly 3 million over the last thirty-five years, and are expected to increase by a further 1,600,000 by the twenty-first century. Their proportion of the total may by then be somewhat smaller (11·4 per cent) than at present (12·3 per cent), but would still be much larger than the 1931 proportion (7·4 per cent). In a very rough and ready way, therefore, it can be said (ignoring present sex differences in working ages and possible future changes in working ages) that the numbers of those below and above working age taken together will probably have substantially increased relatively to those in the conventional working age groups. In this sense, the so-called 'burden of dependency' will have increased.

Not so very long ago it was thought both possible and useful to produce annually a single figure for each country which would summarise all the main factors affecting the future natural increase of population. A great deal of thought went into the study of how such a figure could best be produced, and there were different schools of thought regarding the appropriate way in which the various elements could be combined. It was a common feature of all these 'reproduction rates' that, when the current figure was greater than unity, it meant that the population was more than reproducing itself, whereas when it was less than unity it was failing to reproduce itself. Although such figures are still produced annually in many countries, there is no longer the same confidence in the ability of any such index, however sophisticated its method of calculation, to summarise *all* the factors affecting the future natural increase of population in such a way as to be of real use to the layman. The main reason why these indices have gone out of fashion for this purpose, is that their year-to-year fluctuations at particular times led to exaggerated alternating fears and hopes of declining and expanding populations in the future, so that confidence in the possibility of using a single figure as an indicator of a country's population expectations was badly shaken. It is, as we have seen, quite possible for very large changes in the official forecasts of population to take place in comparatively short periods of time both in respect of the detailed age and sex breakdown and of the totals. But at least these projections can be accompanied by a summary statement of the assumptions on which they are based, and even the layman can, by comparing the assumptions made in different years, understand why such large changes in official expectations have taken place. This is something that no reproduction rate, even when accompanied by a paragraph of explanatory text, could really be expected to do. The reproduction rates, in fact, are no longer regarded as a reliable measure of the implications of current family building habits and mortality for the ultimate replacement of the population.

Regional population projections

Within the framework of the official England and Wales national projection based on the mid-1965 population, and providing figures at intermediate points between now and the year 2001, there are also produced and published official projections for the Standard Regions within England and Wales, though in this case (as with the working population forecasts to be discussed later) 1981 is as far ahead as the forecasts go. The official regional projections based on the *1964* population were used in the 1965 *National Plan*. The current regional projections, based on the *1965* population, differ from, and supersede, those in the *National Plan* in important respects. It should also be noted that the Standard Regions to be discussed in the present section differ from those discussed earlier as a result of changed definitions and titles recently introduced.

The main difficulty in preparing projections for the constituent regions of England and Wales lies, of course, in the appropriate assumptions about the effects of migration. First of all, assumptions have to be made as to how the assumed overall immigration into England and Wales will spread itself amongst the regions. Here the obvious line to take is that the immigrants will spread themselves amongst the regions in roughly the same proportions as they have been doing recently; and the same expectation seems a reasonable assumption with regard to the assumed national *losses* by movement beyond the boundaries of England and Wales. Secondly, recent experience regarding the movement of the *resident* England and Wales population from one region to another can be taken as a broad basis for forecasting future movements, subject to two main provisos.

The first of these provisos relates to planned population overspill and similar arrangements. Where it is already known that there is to be planned dispersal of part of the population of large urban areas to specified areas in a different region, due account ought to be taken both of the scale and of the timing of such plans in forecasting future interregional migration. The second proviso relates to other plans, often of a more tentative character, either to develop the economic resources of particular regions and so arrest part of the traditional emigration from those areas, and perhaps even reverse it, or to impose further restrictions on development in areas which have hitherto had a magnetic attraction in the matter of population movement. In both these connections, those responsible for the regional population projections have naturally consulted the recently established Regional Economic Planning Councils and Boards about future proposals and expectations. Though they have taken these views into account, however, it has not always been possible to accept the figures suggested by the regions in full, since to have done so would have meant that the combined regional totals exceeded the projected national totals within which the regional projections had to be fitted.

Table 7 shows how the official regional projections up to 1981, based on the 1965 population, take into account the migration factor. It will be seen that, within the assumed net international immigration into England and Wales already discussed, the distribution of the immigrants as between the new Standard Regions is broadly in line with what has already been happening in recent years. The assumed decline in net national immigration into England and Wales means, however, that certain regions, notably South-East England and the West Midlands, which are assumed to bear the brunt of the decline just as they bore the brunt of the previous expansion, will have smaller increases by this type of migration in the future than they are now having. (Yorkshire and Humberside, North-West England and the East Midlands are also assumed to be affected in the same way, but the individual absolute numbers involved are smaller than in the case of the two regions just mentioned.)

With regard to interregional movement *within* England and Wales, the biggest absolute variations in the projected movements, by comparison with recent experience, occur in the East Midlands and East Anglia, where relatively large increases in net immigration are anticipated, largely as a result of London's overspill, but also as a result of movements from Birmingham and Sheffield. Overspill is also a major factor explaining why the net outflow from the South-East Region is expected to increase by some 10,000 annually. In the case of the Northern Region, a reduction in the net annual outflow from the recent rate of 7,000 a year to a projected rate of only 3,000 has been assumed to meet, at least in part, the views expressed by the Northern Economic Planning Council. In the Yorkshire and Humberside Region, on the other hand, it is assumed that the current net interregional outflow of 4,000 a year will be doubled in the 1970s.

Annual migration rates past and projected: Standard Regions England and Wales (thousand persons per year)

TABLE 7

	Net interregional movement within England and Wales			Net international movement (including that from Scotland and Ireland)			Net population increase or decrease through population movement		
	1962-65	1964-71	1971-81	1962-65	1964-71	1971-81	1962-65	1964-71	1971-81
Northern England	− 7	− 4	− 3	− 4	− 4	− 4	− 11	− 8	− 7
Yorkshire and Humberside	− 4	− 6	− 8	0	0	− 1	− 4	− 6	− 9
North-West England	− 6	− 6	− 6	− 1	− 1	− 2	− 7	− 7	− 8
East Midlands	+ 5	+ 9	+ 13	+ 3	+ 3	+ 2	+ 8	+ 12	+ 15
West Midlands	− 3	− 4	− 4	+ 11	+ 8	+ 4	+ 8	+ 4	0
East Anglia	+ 9	+ 18	+ 14	+ 2	0	0	+ 11	+ 18	+ 14
South-East England	− 23	− 33	− 32	+ 44	+ 43	+ 31	+ 21	+ 10	− 1
South-West England	+ 26	+ 23	+ 23	− 4	− 5	− 5	+ 22	+ 18	+ 18
Wales	+ 3	+ 3	+ 3	− 3	− 3	− 3	0	0	0
England and Wales	—	—	—	+ 48	+ 41	+ 22	+ 48	+ 41	+ 22

Source. General Register Office, 'Revised projections of the regional distribution of the United Kingdom population in 1971 and 1981', *Economic Trends*, November 1966.

This is partly because of anticipated urban overspill from the cities of York and Sheffield to areas which, though relatively near at hand, happen to come into a different region. For the remaining regions of England and Wales recent experience of net interregional movements has been assumed to continue in much the same way.

The net effect of these various migration assumptions relating to international movement (including that from Scotland and Ireland), and interregional movement within England and Wales, is shown in the last section of Table 7. There it can be seen that the combined effect of the planned dispersal of London's overspill, and the expected decline in immigration from outside the British Isles and from Scotland and Ireland, will have the startling result for the South-East Region of changing a net population *increase* of some 21,000 a year to a net population *decrease* of 1,000 a year. Another area of traditional gain by population movement, the West Midlands Region, from being a net importer of 8,000 people a year will, if the expectations are fulfilled, only break even by the 1970s. The traditional areas of net migration loss, the Northern, Yorkshire and Humberside, and the North-West Regions, are expected to remain in this category. And some of the regions gaining by migration (the South-West, East Anglia and the East-Midlands Regions) are expected to continue to gain either at an increased or only slightly reduced rate.

General manpower forecasts

An interesting example of how the official population projections can form the basis of more specialised forecasting is provided by the case of manpower. The official United Kingdom population projection from the mid-1965 estimate includes detailed age and sex breakdowns for points intermediate between the present day and the end of this century; and in official manpower forecasting there is a natural reluctance to look further ahead than fifteen years or so. Those responsible for suggesting what the *working* population is likely to be between now and 1981 take the projected numbers in the different age and sex groups arrived at on the natality, mortality and migration assumptions we have already discussed, and make a set of further assumptions specifically related to the future manpower position. First, there is the question of future numbers of young men and young women likely to remain in full-time education above the present school-leaving age of 15. It is assumed that, from the summer of 1971 onwards, there will be no further fifteen-year-old entrants to the labour market because of the implementation of promises to raise the school-leaving age to 16. Apart from compulsion to stay at school, however, there has for a long time been a steadily increasing tendency for those in the age groups above the school-leaving age voluntarily to remain in full-time education. Official forecasts of the proportion of young men and young women in each age group expected to remain in full-time education in each of the next years were obtained from the appropriate authorities. But instead of excluding the *whole* number of such stayers-on from the projected working population, only a proportion has been; thus of the 15–19 age group (16–19 from 1972 onwards) expected to remain in full-time education, $87\frac{1}{2}$ per cent of the young men and 75 per cent of the unmarried young women are excluded from the manpower forecasts, but the remainder (although working only part-time or during vacations) are included as full units; and of the 20–24 age group expected to stay on in schools and colleges, only half the men and 40 per cent of the unmarried women are excluded from the projected working population.

A second group of assumptions that had to be made, related to the proportion of women in each age group likely to be married, since this would influence their willingness or ability to take paid employment. On the basis of the increased marriage intensity of recent years it was estimated that the proportion of women of working age who were married would have increased by 1981 to some two-thirds. The third group of assumptions related to the 'activity rates' of the men, the single, divorced and widowed women, and the married women (other than those excluded as being in full-time education) in each age group. The 'activity rate' here means the proportion of the population of any one of these three types (e.g. married women) in a given age group forming (or expected to form) part of the *working* population. On the basis of past trends and the present position in respect of such activity rates, expected future rates were arrived at for each of the three categories for each five-year age group in the 25 and over age-band (including, of course, those in the 60 and over and 65 and over categories). Amongst married women in the 55–59 age group, for example, of whom somewhat less than 39 per cent are at present in the working population, the proportion is expected to rise to 44 per cent by 1971, 48 per cent by 1976 and 52 per cent by 1981. Not all categories are expected to show *increased* activity rates between now and 1981, however. In the case of men over 65, for example, it is suggested that the combined effect of improved pension arrangements and the changing age distribution of the group would be likely to result in a gradual *decline* in activity rates; for men aged 65–69 the assumption is a decline from the present proportion in the working population of 38 per cent to only $30\frac{1}{2}$ per cent by 1981. Everyone admits, of course, that the likelihood of forecasts being falsified even in as short a period as fifteen years is much greater in matters such as activity rates than it is for most of the demographic factors so far considered (except possibly for the migration factor).

A third group of assumptions that had to be made related to changing pressure in the *demand* for labour. It is obvious that, particularly in the case of young people, married women, and those over pensionable age, decisions to take paid employment or not, tend to be influenced by fluctuations in the intensity of the demand for labour. Underlying the assumed activity rates already discussed there had, therefore, to be some assumption about changes in this factor. It was decided to assume that, throughout the next fifteen years, pressure of demand would remain constant at the fairly high level obtaining in 1964 and 1965. There are, however, bound in practice to be year-to-year fluctuations in this pressure, even if it remains relatively stable in the long term. To that extent, the full working population expected even during the next few years *could* fail to materialise.

The combined result of applying assumptions of all these types to the current United Kingdom position is to suggest an increase in the working population of 954,000 in the fifteen-year period 1966–81 (448,000 men and 506,000 women). But because of the effects of the falling annual number of births in the years following the 'bulge' in births in 1946 and 1947, the working population is not expected to show any material increase between now and 1971; and thereafter, for three or four years, the effect of raising the school-leaving age is likely to be an actual *decline* (the first impact will be to remove some 200,000 young people from the labour market). Nearly all the projected increase between now and 1981 is therefore concentrated in the period after 1975. From 1976 onwards there is expected to be a steady rise in male manpower. On the female side of the account the corresponding increase is the combined result of an overall growth in the number of women, an increase in the proportion of them who are likely to be married (which, of course, *reduces* the likelihood of their seeking paid employment), and an expected increase in the activity rates of married women.

Although, as we have seen, the number of women in the working population is expected to increase by some 506,000 by 1981, because a much higher proportion of this larger total will consist of *married* women, and because many of them will not want, or be able to engage in paid employment on a regular or full-time basis, the number of full-time working women may actually decrease (the figure nevertheless implies a substantial increase in womanpower). Finally, although the future age structure of the working population is affected by demographic factors, by the expected raising of the school-leaving age, by the increasing tendency to stay in full-time education, and by changing activity rates, it is interesting to notice that the proportion of our manpower under 40 is expected to remain much as it is at present (slightly over half) for the next fifteen years.

Skilled manpower forecasts

Just as those forecasting the future working population have to take the officially projected population and add to the demographic assumptions a further set of assumptions needed for this more specialised purpose, so those attempting to predict the future supply of people possessing particular types of skill or training have also to grapple with the problems of formulating assumptions specific to their particular needs. To illustrate the special difficulties involved in forecasting supply in such cases, the example of school teaching can be taken. One of the first difficulties arising here relates to the variety of original routes of entry into school teaching. For, in addition to those who have successfully completed a course of teacher-training (either with or without having previously taken a university degree), there are non-graduate entrants without such training, whose employment is limited and temporary in character, and graduate entrants, who may teach indefinitely without specific teacher-training. In each of these groups there are both men and women, and the alternative occupations and professions open to the different groups and to the two sexes show considerable variation at any one time. There are also the variations over time to be taken into account, for relative salaries and prospects within the range of alternative occupations open to potential teachers are in a constant state of flux, and it is extremely difficult to predict their

83

future pattern. A recent study of the attitudes of undergraduates towards teaching as a possible career suggested that, in the Faculties of Arts, Social Science and Pure Science, not more than a quarter of the final-year students were firmly committed to school-teaching, which inevitably has to depend for its ultimate share on attracting some of the uncommitted-to-teaching (whether through failure to achieve their first choice of career, or through a change of preference).

Formidable as this list of difficulties may already seem, however, there still remains to be tackled a group of even more difficult assumptions, namely those relating to 'wastage' and possible subsequent return to teaching, full-time or part-time. Assumptions regarding the future numbers of places on teacher-training courses of different types, and the future relative attractions of teaching as against other careers to those in their teens and early twenties, only deal with one part of the future supply position. This still leaves the expectation of attracting new recruits to training later in life to be considered. And it also leaves out of account the loss to teaching of those whose training is abandoned, or who fail; and those who, after successfully completing a course of training, never teach at all; and the subsequent dropping-out of more and more teachers (particularly women), together with the return to teaching of those who, trained or otherwise, have previously taught. One way of providing at least a tentative basis for formulating assumptions on some of these questions is by looking at the behaviour in these respects of recent 'cohorts' of women entrants to teaching, and finding out what they have done between their first entry to this career and the present time. This was done recently with a large and carefully selected sample of women entering teaching at different dates and after various types of teacher-training (including graduation without subsequent training). Of every 100 young women who went straight into what was then a two-year teacher-training after leaving school, and successfully completed the course in 1950, six never subsequently taught at all. Five years later only seventy of the original 100 were still in pensionable teaching service; and five years later still, only forty-two were. Of those missing, about two were either in *non-pensionable* teaching or in occupations ancillary to teaching. Of the original 100, therefore, fifty-six had, ten years later, been lost to teaching in the widest sense, either temporarily or permanently.

It can be argued, of course, that in cases of this type the number of people 'missing' at a particular date is not an ideal means of measuring 'wastage'. For many purposes it is more meaningful to calculate man- or woman-years of service given by a particular cohort of entrants, and to relate this to the maximum that could have been given by that cohort if there had been no 'wastage' at all. If, for example, we take the same group of two-year-trained women teachers who started to teach. ˙050 (but this time only include in the calculation those who subsequently gave *some* teaching service, however little), a calculation of this kind will show that the loss of potential teaching service by this cohort in the first ten years or so after beginning their service was 29 per cent. For future manpower estimates of the type at present under discussion, however, the cruder measure of those from a particular cohort of entrants missing or in service at different intervals of time is the more appropriate 'wastage' measure to use.

This dropping out of teaching was, of course, mainly due to more of the women concerned marrying, and to their marrying at younger ages than had happened with their predecessors. If these tendencies continue to increase in the immediate future as they have increased in the immediate past, appropriate 'wastage' rates can be assumed for future cohorts of women entering teaching at each stage of their lives. In making assumptions about the possible return to teaching after marrying and, partially or completely, bringing up a family, we have to rely on data from the same survey relating to prewar cohorts of entry and their postwar behaviour in returning or not returning to teaching, full-time or part-time, for short periods or long. And an estimate has also to be made of the future measures likely to be taken (ranging from tax concessions to school timetable adjustments to suit the teaching mother) to encourage more married women to return to teaching, and the probable success of the predicted combination of such measures in achieving their object. Bodies such as the National Advisory Council on the Training and Supply of Teachers can hardly be blamed if, faced with almost overwhelming difficulties of the kinds discussed, the forecasts they have made both of teacher supply and wastage have sometimes been falsified by events. The range and specificity of information needed in order to arrive at reasonable assumptions in attempting to estimate the future supply of those possessing particular vocational skills and/or training is such as often to make them subject to margins of error on an altogether different scale from those applying to short-term projections of the population at large or even the working population in general.

Theories

Although the germ of a population theory can be found in writings of much earlier date, it was Malthus who not only formulated a theory of inherent population tendencies, but illustrated and supported it by a mass of evidence from the history of many countries. The essence of his theory can be quite briefly stated. Man's power to produce population is greater than his power to produce subsistence. Indeed, so great is the first of these powers that, if left unchecked (a situation inconceivable in practice) a population could double itself every twenty-five years, thus increasing in a geometrical ratio; while the second power seemed unlikely, at best, to make possible more than a subsistence increase in an arithmetical ratio. Leaving aside these particular ratios, the second of which proved particularly difficult to validate, the proposition of an inherently greater capacity of populations than of food supplies to grow, seemed on the face of it highly probable. The consequent chronic tendency for population to outrun the means of subsistence is, said Malthus, held in check by vice and misery; by what he also called the 'preventive' checks, operating to reduce the birth rate, and the 'positive' checks, operating to raise the death rate.

Obviously a better way of holding the tendency in check was by moral restraint, postponement of marriage until one could afford to bring up a family. Except in Ireland, where after the famine of 1845–47 there was a unique combination of very low marriage rates, large families and virtual absence of family planning, and large-scale emigration, the Malthusian way out of the population dilemma has not been widely adopted. In Britain (as in other European countries) family limitation by birth control has taken the place of the moral restraint advocated by Malthus. And this, together with the export of both people and capital, our emergence as the 'workshop of the world', and the opening up of the New World as a source of agricultural products and raw materials, has, as everyone knows, provided an alternative means of escape.

The Malthusian picture of population always tending to increase beyond the available means of subsistence, and being brought back to the earlier level by the preventive and positive checks and by moral restraint, seems to imply oscillation of numbers around a particular figure. Britain's experience over the last century and a half does not, of course, fit this particular pattern. Moreover, the idea that stability of numbers is ever likely to come about of itself, or that it could be achieved by deliberate policy, is not widely supported today. Inherent instability, rather than stability, seems, at least so far as contemporary populations are concerned, to be their probable feature. For even comparatively small changes in fertility, mortality or migration, are likely to bring about alterations in the age and sex structure of a population which will take some time to work themselves through and out of that population while, in the course of their progress, overall population numbers can hardly fail to change in one direction or another.

The doubtful relevance of Malthus's theories to Britain's present population situation does not, of course, imply that they lack relevance anywhere. Many countries in Asia and elsewhere have found that, as a result of spectacular reductions in mortality, the means of subsistence are proving quite insufficient for their needs, and are having to attempt to control population increase by widespread programmes of family planning. The attempted solution may not be in accordance with what Malthus himself advocated, but the factors in the situation are basically those to which he drew attention. Not long ago, as a result of detailed studies on the spot by a distinguished team from the London School of Economics, it was shown how well some of the dominant features in the desperate situation of the island of Mauritius (few natural resources, little scope for investment, and, since the elimination of malaria and other public health improvements, one of the highest rates of natural increase in the world) accorded with the Malthusian outline.

Britain also gave birth to another, and more recent, population concept, that of an 'optimum' population. What was involved here was a means of judging, in purely economic terms, whether a country was over- or under-populated. Edwin Cannan first suggested late in the nineteenth century that, as overloading of one factor of production by others produced diminishing returns, the most advantageous size of population for any country was that which produced the maximum return per head, both larger and smaller numbers being likely to produce a smaller *per capita* return, and to be evidence of over- and under-population respectively. Cannan himself was the first to admit that the practical application of this idea to any particular country's situation was fraught with difficulty. For one thing, inventions and their application would obviously alter the optimum. Again, unless a particular country's economy was completely isolated from the rest of the world, great care was needed in handling the elements in making any such estimate. In the event, the 'optimum' concept has not been widely adopted as a guide to population policy, partly because of the difficulty that, by the time it was realised that the optimum point had been either reached or passed, technological change might well have altered the whole future situation. Attention has tended to shift to the current rate of growth or decline of a country's population, and to trying to weigh up the favourable and unfavourable aspects, political and social as well as purely economic, of the rates of growth or decline currently being experienced and being forecast.

There remains one further type of possible population tendency which must be discussed at greater length, because it cannot be adequately dealt with in a sentence or two. This is the possibility of a decline in the national level of intelligence. Let it be said at once that the decision to include discussion of this particular possibility in no way implies acceptance of the view that what is measured by so-called intelligence tests is either a unitary trait 'intelligence', or comprises a more important set of abilities than any other set. It merely arises from the two circumstances that a belief in the likelihood of such a decline has gained wide currency, and that the supposed foundation for such a belief lies in the differential fertility of the various social class groups to which attention has been drawn earlier.

It has already been shown that there is a social class gradient in fertility, the size of family tending to get larger as one descends the social scale; though the gradient is not an unbroken one, since the least fertile group is not the top one, but comprises the salaried employees, the 'unproductive clerks'. It is also the case that the mean score in intelligence tests of children in large families is significantly lower than the mean score of children in small families; and that this difference applies throughout the range of family sizes. This negative correlation between the *size* of a family and the average intelligence test performance of its members, may be associated with a number of factors—less experience in the use of words resulting from having more brothers and sisters and therefore less need to communicate with adults; a less favourable adult home environment for intellectual development in the humbler home; a poorer inheritance of the skills measured by intelligence tests from parents themselves ill-equipped with these skills.

These last two possible factors are central to the now somewhat barren but once popular nature-nurture controversy. Though some psychologists still believe that the middle classes possess a basic intellectual superiority and are able to maintain it by selective mating and a marked tendency to inherit these traits, the view is widely held that not more than half of the observed variation in the measured intelligence of children is genetic in origin. If this is so, environmental improvements resulting from social progress may substantially reduce both the speed and scale of the 'expected' decline in the national level of measured intelligence. There are, moreover, several other possible mitigating factors. One of these is the fact that, at the upper end of the social scale, family size (as already stated) actually increases as social status rises. Moreover, two large-scale investigations of Scottish eleven-year olds in 1932 and 1947 showed that in this fifteen-year period, the mean level of measured intelligence amongst those in that age group has shown not a fall, but a slight rise.

There are, of course, very many unknown elements that could easily influence the final result. How, for example, do the bachelors and spinsters and the childless couples differ in measured intelligence from the rest of the adult population? And it must be remembered that we have virtually no measured intelligence data for adults in any case, whether parents or not; their relative situation in this matter is merely inferred from the social status of the jobs held by the adult males. Finally, the serious limitation of the tests, on the results of which the negative correlation between family size and measured intelligence is based, suggest that, at worst, there has been shown to be a possible danger of some future national reduction in a small fraction out of a multiplicity of abilities and aptitudes.

A population policy?

It is natural, finally, to ask two questions. What ought Britain's aims to be, in population terms? And what would be the appropriate policies to achieve these aims? To take the first of these questions, we are obviously not in the situation in which some countries find themselves, where everyone is agreed that unchecked population growth needs, in the national interest, to be drastically curtailed. Indeed, we have only just emerged from a phase in which the possible dangers of a *declining* population were looming large; and it is difficult for the public mind to adjust itself at such short notice to thinking in terms of a possibly too rapid *expansion* of numbers. Nevertheless, it is quite possible to argue that, for a variety of reasons, the expected increase in the size of our population in the next thirty-five years or so is too large to be satisfactory. For one thing, the resources we should have to devote to housing these additional numbers might prevent us from achieving other, perhaps more desirable objectives. Again, the amount of land required for housing on this scale could mean too great a sacrifice in agricultural or amenity terms. Yet again, the traffic implications of such a population increase might be too grave to make it acceptable. Warnings of these and other types have already come from physical planners and from those concerned with agriculture, but they have tended to be sporadic and uncoordinated.

As yet Governments, too, seem to have contented themselves with expressing satisfaction (at least until recently) that people have been tending to have slightly larger families, and have falsified earlier fears of population decline; they have not suggested any clear national aims in this respect. Instead, they have concentrated on the *regional* aspects of the matter, where there is a fair measure of agreement between the main political parties as to what changes in past internal migration trends it would be desirable to bring about. On a national level, recent Governments have tended to suggest that it is a pity our own people are emigrating on the present scale, and to hope that the propensity to emigrate will decline; to say that we must not admit more Commonwealth immigrants than can be successfully assimilated; and to leave it at that.

There is, however, one aspect of growth in numbers on which something approaching unanimity is beginning to emerge, and that is the question of empowering and encouraging local authorities to provide family planning advice and facilities on social, and not merely on medical grounds. The debate in the House of Commons on 17 February 1967, when a Private Member's National Health Service (Family Planning) Bill was given an unopposed Second Reading, made it clear that there was fairly general agreement on a number of issues. First, that significant numbers of parents (as had been shown in a recent Gallup poll) were finding themselves with larger families than they wanted to have, so that there was a need on this account alone to provide better advice and facilities for family planning, in order that achieved family sizes should more nearly approach the parentally-desired ones. Secondly, that some other parents, not appreciating the extent to which large families even today could mean poverty, had more children than, had they realised these implications, they would have done. Thirdly, that there was also a minority who were too feckless, ignorant or indifferent to their family and social responsibilities to be influenced by the consideration that the bearing of children was not, as Mr Houghton observed, purely a personal matter. In the light of these considerations, empowering local health authorities to provide advice free of charge (and free contraceptives for those who could not afford to pay)

[margin note: Dr Edwin Brooks M.P.]

wherever it was socially necessary, instead of being restricted to medical grounds alone, seemed the least that needed to be done.

Recent studies such as *The Poor and the Poorest* by Professors Townsend and Abel-Smith, have reinforced these arguments by showing children to be in poverty in contemporary Britain on a scale previously unsuspected. For though the immediate aim had to be to do something for these children, by greatly improved family allowances and in other ways, one obvious further implication was that better family planning could have prevented some of this hardship and suffering in the first place.

If and when a more positive national population policy is decided upon, what measures are available to British Governments to bring about the desired result? In certain respects, powers of control seem perfectly adequate. In the matter of immigration, for example, the 1962 legislation would appear to provide all that anyone could ask for to prevent the inflow of Commonwealth citizens exceeding what is acceptable. On the other hand, public opinion would probably be unfavourable towards a corresponding provision for the control of *emigration*, though present and future Governments might well wish that they could influence that side of the migration account equally directly and effectively. Control of *internal* migration within the United Kingdom, has, of course, to be by indirect means rather than by direct action, whether that migration takes the form of movement from, say, Scotland or Northern Ireland to England, or of movement from one region of England and Wales to another. Although the 1961 Census provided, for the first time, reliable information (on a 10 per cent sample basis) on the amount and direction of such movement in the year 1960–61, and the 1966 Census will provide similar information (also on a 10 per cent sample basis) for a *longer* time span, people have only been asked whether they moved and, if so, whence and whither. The vital missing information relates to *why* they moved; and it is arguable that, however complex their reasons may sometimes be, without some reliable data on this point, Government action to counter existing internal migration trends in appropriate cases is severely handicapped; though the obvious reasons (the availability of attractive employment opportunities and social amenities) may not be in much doubt.

It is on the family-building side that both the knowledge as to why people act as they do, and the means of persuading them to modify their actions, seem to be at their weakest. It is no secret, for example, that the 'boom in babies' in 1956 and subsequent years came as a complete surprise both to demographers and others. No one had forecast a development of this kind on this scale, and *ex post facto* explanations as to why it happened, and as to the chances of the trend either continuing or being reversed, are by no means convincing. Yet if Governments do not know why a fashion for larger families develops, or how long it is likely to last, how are they to judge which factors will be likely to foster or discourage such a development? Increases in State family allowances, and in income-tax allowances for children, may help to reduce the differential economic hardships to which fathers of large families are subject, in the lower and middle income ranges respectively; but no one is in a position to say, even in the broadest terms, how effectively they operate in actually bringing into being children who would not otherwise have been born. Moreover, the more we try to help the parents of *existing* large families by such means, the more we could be encouraging future family size increases; and the latter may, in our present population circumstances, be the last thing we want to do. A major programme of research is clearly needed both into the factors influencing parents in their family-building and into the probable effects of different measures of State policy.

References and further reading

(Place of publication is London except where otherwise indicated.)

CURRENT, OR MOST RECENT, OFFICIAL PUBLISHED SOURCES
OF BRITISH DEMOGRAPHIC DATA

General Register Office, London
(All publications listed in this section relate mainly to England and Wales
unless otherwise stated.)
Registrar General's Weekly Return
Registrar General's Quarterly Return
Registrar General's Annual Estimate of the Population
Registrar General's Statistical Review (separate volumes of tables, com-
mentary, supplements: annual)
Registrar General's Decennial Supplement to the Census (separate
volumes on types of mortality)
Census 1961:
    County Reports
    County Tables for Occupation, Industry, Socio-Economic Group
    Preliminary Report
    Classification of Occupations
    Age, Marital Condition, and General Tables
    Report on Welsh-speaking Population
    Birthplace and Nationality Tables
    Scientific and Technological Qualifications (Great Britain)
    Commonwealth Immigrants in the Conurbations
    Education Tables
    Fertility Tables
    Housing Tables
    Industry Tables
    Occupation Tables

Migration Tables
Socio-Economic Group Tables
Usual Residence Tables
Workplace Tables
Household Composition Tables
Also National Summary Tables in many of these cases, some on a Great
Britain basis, as well as Summary Leaflets for separate areas.

Note. The General Register Office, Edinburgh, and the General Register Division of
the Ministry of Finance of the Government of Northern Ireland, publish broadly
corresponding demographic data for Scotland and Northern Ireland respectively.

Royal Commission on Population, 1944–49

Report
Report of the Economics Committee
Reports and Papers of the Statistics Committee
Reports of the Biological and Medical Committee
Report on the Family Census 1946 (D. V. Glass and E. Grebenik, *The
Trend and Pattern of Fertility in Great Britain*)
Report on a Family Limitation Enquiry (E. Lewis-Faning, *Family
Limitation and its Influence on Human Fertility*)
Royal Commission on the Distribution of the Industrial Population, 1937–39
Report (1940, reprinted 1963)

Central Office of Information
Britain, an Official Handbook 1967

Central Statistical Office
Abstract of Regional Statistics (No. 2, 1966)
Annual Abstract of Statistics
List of Principal Statistical Sources . . . (1965) (Studies in Official Statistics,
No. 11)
Monthly Digest of Statistics

Commonwealth Relations Office
Oversea Migration Board: Statistics for 1964 (an annual publication no
longer issued)

Committee on Manpower Resources for Science and Technology
Report on the 1965 Triennial Manpower Survey of Engineers, Technologists, Scientists and Technical Supporting Staff (1966)

Interim Report of the Working Group on Manpower Parameters for Scientific Growth (1966)

Home Office
Commonwealth Immigrants Act 1962: Control of Immigration: Statistics 1966 (1967)

Ministry of Housing and Local Government
Housing Statistics, Great Britain (No. 3, 1966)

Ministry of Labour
Length of Working Life of Males in Great Britain (1959) (Studies in Official Statistics, No. 4)
Material collected by the Ministry of Labour (1958) (Guides to Official Sources, No. 1)
Manpower Studies 1964:
  1. Pattern of the Future
  2. The Metal Industries
  3. The Construction Industry

United Nations
Demographic Yearbook 1965 (1966)

Welsh Office
Digest of Welsh Statistics (No. 12, 1965)

PUBLICATIONS RELEVANT TO INDIVIDUAL CHAPTERS

Introductory, and Chapters 1 and 2
Studies of an introductory nature covering a wide range include the following:
I. Bowen, *Population* (1954)
P. R. Cox, *Demography* (3rd edition, Cambridge 1959)
A. M. Carr-Saunders, D. C. Jones and C. A. Moser, *A Survey of Social Conditions in England and Wales* (3rd edition, Oxford 1956)
D. C. Marsh, *The Changing Social Structure of England and Wales 1871–1961* (2nd edition 1965)
D. H. Wrong, *Population and Society* (New York 1961)
Matters of Life and Death (1958) (General Register Office)

Why a Census? (1961) (General Register Office)
'Vital Statistics in England and Wales: A Survey of Sources and Production' in Commentary Volume of Registrar General's *Statistical Review for 1963*

Chapters 3, 4, 5 and 8

T. Arie, 'Class and disease', *New Society*, 27 January 1966.
T. McKeown and R. G. Record ,'Reasons for the decline of mortality in England and Wales during the nineteenth century', *Population Studies*, Cambridge, November 1962.
C. C. Spicer and L. Lipworth, *Regional and Social Factors in Infant Mortality* (1966) (General Register Office: Studies on Medical and Population Subjects, No. 19)
Maternity in Great Britain (1948) (Population Investigation Committee)
J. W. B. Douglas and J. M. Blomfield, *Children Under Five* (1958)
Infants at Risk (1964) (Office of Health Economics)
N. R. Butler and D. G. Bonham, *Perinatal Mortality* (Edinburgh 1963) (National Birthday Trust Survey)
R. Illsley, 'Social class selection and class differences in relation to still-births and infant deaths', *British Medical Journal*, 24 December 1955.
P. B. Medawar, *The Future of Man* (1960) (B.B.C. Reith Lectures 1959)
J. A. and O. Banks, *Feminism and Family Planning in Victorian England* (Liverpool 1964)
'The Increase in Births since 1955' in Commentary Volume of Registrar General's *Statistical Review for 1962*
G. Rowntree, 'New facts on teenage marriage', *New Society*, 4 October 1962
J. Matras, 'Social strategies of family formation: Data for British female cohorts born 1831–1906', *Population Studies*, Cambridge, November 1965
D. V. Glass, 'Family limitation in Europe: A survey of recent studies', in C. V. Kiser, ed., *Research in Family Planning* (Princeton, N.J. 1962)
D. V. Glass, 'Family planning programmes and action in Western Europe', *Population Studies*, Cambridge, March 1966
G. Rowntree and R. M. Pierce, 'Birth control in Britain', *Population Studies*, Cambridge, July and November 1961

Chapter 6

Commonwealth Immigrants in the Conurbations (Census 1961, England and Wales)

Commonwealth Relations Office *Oversea Migration Board Statistics* (annually for twelve years 1954–65; similar figures, not always identical in form, have appeared recently in the Registrar General's *Return* for the third quarter of each year)

'Migration', in Commentary Volume of Registrar General's *Statistical Review for 1963*

N. H. Carrier and J. R. Jeffery, *External Migration : A study of the available statistics 1815–1950* (1953) (General Register Office: Studies on Medical and Population Subjects, No. 6)

J. Isaac, *British Post-war Migration* (Cambridge 1954)

Chapter 7

Migration Tables (Census 1961, England and Wales)

Volume 8: Internal Migration (Edinburgh, Census 1961, Scotland)

'Migration', in Commentary Volume of Registrar General's *Statistical Review for 1963*

Royal Commission on the Distribution of the Industrial Population, *Report* (1940)

J. A. Rowntree, *Internal Migration* (1957) (General Register Office: Studies on Medical and Population Subjects, No. 11)

R. Illsley, A. Finlayson and B. Thompson, 'The motivation and characteristics of internal migrants in Scotland', *Milbank Memorial Fund Quarterly*, New York, April and July 1963

D. Friedlander and R. J. Roshier, 'A study of internal migrants in England and Wales', *Population Studies*, Cambridge, March and July 1966

A series of papers on different aspects of migration in North-east England has recently been published under the auspices of the Geography Department of the University of Newcastle-on-Tyne under the general title 'Papers on Migration and Mobility . . .'

C. A. Moser and W. Scott, *British Towns* (Edinburgh 1961)

Chapter 9

H. Gavron, *The Captive Wife : Conflicts of Housebound Mothers* (1966)

International Council of Women, *Woman in a Changing World* (1966)

V. Klein, *Britain's Married Women Workers* (1965)

A. Myrdal and V. Klein, *Women's Two Roles* (1956)

Women in Britain (1964) (Central Office of Information Reference Pamphlet No. 67)

Women and Work (1965) (Symposium based on B.B.C. Home Service Broadcasts)

M. P. Banton, *The Coloured Quarter* (1955)

M. P. Banton, *White and Coloured* (1959)

R. B. Davison, *West Indian Migrants* (1962)

R. B. Davison, *Commonwealth Immigrants* (1964)

R. B. Davison, *Black British* (1966)

R. Glass, *Newcomers: The West Indians in London* (1960)

A. H. Richmond, *Colour Prejudice in Britain* (1954)

A. H. Richmond, *The Colour Problem* (Harmondsworth 1955)

J. Rex and R. Moore, *Race, Community and Conflict* (1966)

N. Hawkes, *Immigrant Children in British Schools* (1966)

G. E. W. Wolstenholme and M. O'Connor, eds., *Immigration: Medical and Social Aspects* (1967)

D. Cole and J. E. G. Utting, *The Economic Circumstances of Old People* (Welwyn, Herts, 1962)

D. Wedderburn, *Financial Resources Available to Older People* (Cambridge 1965)

B. E. Shenfield, *Social Policies for Old Age* (1957)

Committee on the Economic and Financial Problems of Provision for Old Age, 1953–54, *Report* (1954)

Ministry of Labour, *Employment of Older Men and Women: the Economic and Social Effects of the Increasing Proportion of Older People in the Population* (1952)

Ministry of Labour, *Length of Working Life of Males in Great Britain* (1959) (Studies in Official Statistics, No. 4)

United Nations: Department of Economic and Social Affairs (Bureau of Social Affairs: Population Branch), *The Aging of Populations and its Economic and Social Implications* (New York 1956)

Chapter 10

On general methods of population forecasting, one of the most readable manuals for the layman is the third in the United Nations Department of Economic and Social Affairs Manuals on Methods of Estimating Populations, *Methods for Population Projections by Sex and Age* (New York 1956). On the methods used in recent British national population forecasting, see 'Projecting the population of the United Kingdom', *Economic Trends*, May 1965. For the current U.K. projections themselves, see the April issue of the *Monthly Digest of Statistics* (those for England and Wales can also be found in the Registrar General's *Report* for the 4th quarter of each year). For the projections for the regions of England and Wales from the mid-1965 total population, and the reasons for the assumptions used, see 'Revised projections of the regional distribution of the United Kingdom population in 1971 and 1981', *Economic Trends*, November 1966. Each of the Regional Economic Planning Councils has recently produced a comprehensive report on the present and planned future development of its region in population, manpower and other terms, for example *A Review of Yorkshire and Humberside* (1966)

J. Boreham, 'The pressure of population', *New Society*, 3 March 1966

Chapter 11

Scientific and Technological Qualifications (Census 1961, Great Britain)

'Forecasts of the working population 1966–81', *Ministry of Labour Gazette*, November 1966

B. C. Roberts and J. H. Smith, ed., *Manpower Policy and Employment Trends* (1966)

Committee on Manpower Resources for Science and Technology, *A Review of the Scope and Problems of Scientific and Technological Manpower Policy* (1965)

H.R.H. Prince Philip, Duke of Edinburgh, 'What Next?', *New Scientist*, 24 November 1966.

Department of Education and Science, *The Demand for and Supply of Teachers 1963–1986* (1965) (9th Report of National Advisory Council on the Training and Supply of Teachers)

Problems Facing the Teaching Profession (P.E.P. Broadsheet, November 1966)

R. K. Kelsall, *Women and Teaching* (1963)

Chapter 12

A. Dick, 'The founder of modern demography', *New Society*, 17 February 1966

D. V. Glass ed., *Introduction to Malthus* (1953)

D. E. C. Eversley, *Social Theories of Fertility and the Malthusian Debate* (Oxford 1959)

W. B. Reddaway, *Economics of a Declining Population* (1939)

A. Carter, *Too Many People?* (1962) (Fabian Research Series No. 232)

D. V. Glass, 'Fertility and birth control in developed societies, and some questions of policy for less developed societies' in *Proceedings of the 7th Conference of the International Planned Parenthood Federation* (Amsterdam 1964)

E

D. V. Glass, 'Population growth, fertility and population policy', *The Advancement of Science*, November 1960

G. F. McCleary, *The Malthusian Population Theory* (1953)

B. Abel-Smith and P. Townsend, *The Poor and the Poorest* (1965)

R. M. Titmuss and B. Abel-Smith, *Social Policies and Population Growth in Mauritius* (1961)

Appendix 1:
Standard Regions of England and Wales

Northern
Cumberland
Durham
Northumberland
Westmorland
Yorkshire, N.R.

East and West Ridings
Yorkshire, E.R.
Yorkshire, W.R.

North-Western
Cheshire
Derbyshire, part of
   Lancashire

North Midland
Derbyshire, part of
   Leicestershire
Lincolnshire
   Parts of Holland
   Parts of Kesteven
   Parts of Lindsey
Northamptonshire
Nottinghamshire
Peterborough, Soke of
Rutland

Midland
Herefordshire
Shropshire
Staffordshire
Warwickshire
Worcestershire

Eastern
Bedfordshire
Cambridgeshire
Ely, Isle of
Essex, part of
Hertfordshire, part of
Huntingdonshire
Norfolk
Suffolk, East
Suffolk, West

London and South Eastern
Essex, part of
Hertfordshire, part of
Kent
London A.C.
Middlesex
Surrey
Sussex, East
Sussex, West

Southern
Berkshire
Buckinghamshire
Dorset, part of
Hampshire
Oxfordshire
Wight, Isle of

South Western
Cornwall
Devon
Dorset, part of
Gloucestershire
Somerset
Wiltshire

Wales I (South West)
Breconshire
Carmarthenshire
Glamorgan
Monmouthshire

Wales II (Remainder)
Anglesey
Caernarvonshire
Cardiganshire
Denbighshire
Flintshire
Merionethshire
Montgomeryshire
Pembrokeshire
Radnorshire

REVISED STANDARD REGIONS, 1965 AND LATER

North
Cumberland
Durham
Northumberland
Westmorland
Yorkshire, N.R.

Yorkshire and Humberside
Lincolnshire
  Parts of Lindsey, part of
Yorkshire, E.R.
Yorkshire, W.R.

North West
Cheshire
Derbyshire, part of
Lancashire

East Midlands
Derbyshire, part of
Leicestershire
Lincolnshire
  Parts of Holland
  Parts of Kesteven
  Parts of Lindsey, part of
Northamptonshire
Nottinghamshire
Rutland

West Midlands
Herefordshire
Shropshire
Staffordshire
Warwickshire
Worcestershire

East Anglia
Cambridgeshire and Isle of Ely
Huntingdon and Peterborough
Norfolk
Suffolk, East
Suffolk, West

South East
Bedfordshire
Berkshire
Buckinghamshire
Dorset, part of
Essex
Greater London
Hampshire
Hertfordshire
Kent
Oxfordshire
Surrey
Sussex, East
Sussex, West
Wight, Isle of

South West
Cornwall
Devon
Dorset, part of
Gloucestershire
Somerset
Wiltshire

Wales I (South East)
Breconshire
Carmarthenshire
Glamorgan
Monmouthshire

Wales II (Remainder)
Anglesey
Caernarvonshire
Cardiganshire
Denbighshire
Flintshire
Merionethshire
Montgomeryshire
Pembrokeshire
Radnorshire

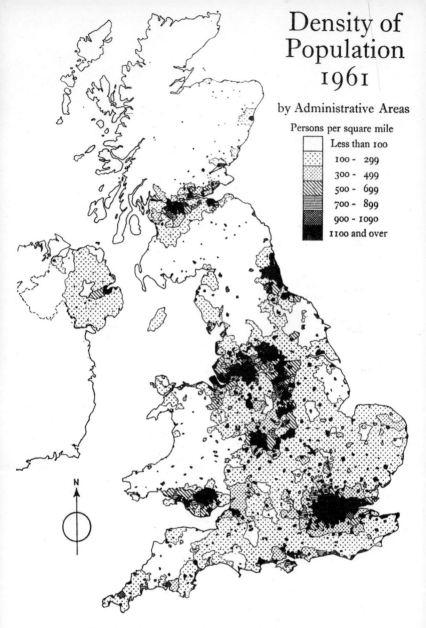

Density of
Population
1961

by Administrative Areas

Persons per square mile

Less than 100
100 - 299
300 - 499
500 - 699
700 - 899
900 - 1090
1100 and over

N

Reproduced by courtesy of the Central Office of Information

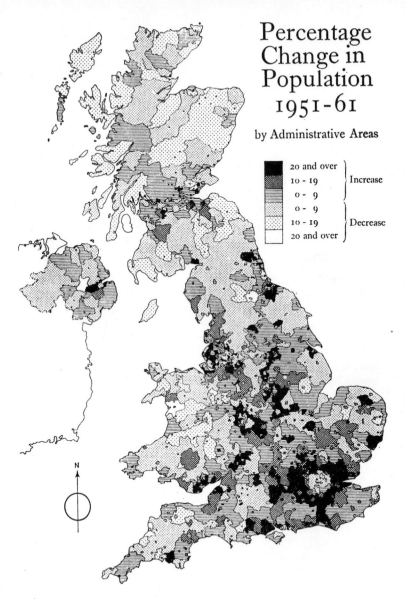

Percentage Change in Population 1951-61

by Administrative Areas

20 and over	Increase
10 - 19	
0 - 9	
0 - 9	Decrease
10 - 19	
20 and over	

N

Reproduced by courtesy of the Central Office of Information

Appendix 2:
Some very recent developments

As a 1972 edition has been called for, some of the new data becoming available and the new developments taking place in the period since this book was first published in 1967 may be discussed.

Fertility and mortality

The fall in the annual number of live births, first taking place in 1965, has continued in the seven years since then, the England and Wales figures for 1965–71 being around 862,700, 849,800, 832,200, 819,300, 797,500, 784,500 and a provisionally estimated 783,000 (the final 1971 figure not yet being available). There were signs of the beginning of an upward movement when, in the last quarter of 1970, the numbers proved to be some 8,300 greater than in the corresponding quarter of the previous year, and this tendency was maintained with almost exactly the same margin in the first quarter of 1971. By the second quarter the margin had narrowed considerably, and in the final two quarters of 1971 the decline as compared with 1970 reasserted itself. And taking the full years 1970 and 1971 the downward trend has not yet been arrested.

One factor of probable relevance to this very recent and short-lived upturn in births is so-called 'pill fright' on the part of some women (and/or their husbands) as a result of the December 1969 advice from the chairman of the Scowen Committee on safety of drugs, that they should check whether the brand of contraceptive pill they were using was one of the 19 (out of 36) which doctors were now being asked *not* to prescribe because of thrombosis risk. An upturn of the size indicated occurring in the last quarter of 1970 and being maintained in the next quarter as well, would seem to indicate a natural reaction to this alarming news. An increase in births lasting for a number of years was certainly expected to take place when the girl babies born in the immediate post-war 'bulge' years 1946 and 1947 reached child-bearing ages. They are now, of course, in their mid-twenties, but the expected birth increase has not materialised.

A major new development of the period since this book was first published has been the passing of the Abortion Act which, while not providing 'abortion on demand' as advocated by some, nevertheless very greatly widened the circumstances in which such operations could legally be performed. Over 54,000 abortions were notified in England and Wales in 1969, the first full year after the Act came into force in April 1968. In 1970 the number was nearly 84,000 and it has risen to a figure of nearly 127,000 in 1971. Indeed, if the rate in the final quarter of 1971 were maintained throughout a full year it would mean some 153,000 registered abortions annually. Viewed alongside annual recorded births of only around 780,000 this naturally raises the very controversial question as to what is an acceptable level of abortion for England and Wales. One point worth noting is that nearly half these registered pregnancy terminations relate to single women, so that figures of illegitimate births are bound to decline as those of abortions increase; currently some 83 of every thousand recorded births are illegitimate.

Turning to mortality, the downward trend in infant mortality rates has continued, though at a decreasing pace, the figures being: 19 for each of the years 1965 and 1966; 18·3 for 1967 and 1968; and 18·0, 18·2 and 17·6 for 1969, 1970 and 1971. Life expectancy at birth has increased by roughly a further year since page 26 was written, the England and Wales figures for the three-year period 1968–70 being 68·6 years for males and 74·9 for females.

Social class variations in mortality

New and rather unfavourable light has very recently been shed on the question of the social class gradient in *general* mortality. It has already been explained in chapter 8 how the provisional estimates for standard (or standardised) mortality ratios by social class for the period around the 1951 Census had appeared to mark the end of the depressing linkage between one's mortality experience and one's position in the social hierarchy; but how, when certain adjustments had been unofficially made, the W-effect disappeared and a gradient of the old type reasserted itself. The publication of the Occupational Mortality Tables in the *Decennial Supplement* to the England and Wales Census 1961, eagerly awaited (p. 53) towards the end of 1967, did not in fact take place until four years later, just before Christmas 1971. The new evidence now provided makes several things clear. First, the official *adjusted* ratios for males for 1949–53 (86, 92, 101, 104, 118) show a gradient steeper than both the unofficially adjusted ratios for that period quoted earlier in the present book, *and* the agreed ratios for 1930–32. Secondly, the figures now published for the first time for 1959–63 (78, 81, 100, 103, 143) show the difference in mortality experience at the two ends of the social scale to be very much greater now than it was ten years before, and also very much larger than it had been thirty and even forty years earlier. The Registrar General warns us that too much reliance must not be placed on these ratios, for 'it is impossible to disentangle real differential changes in mortality from apparent differences due to changes in classification'. Even when due weight is given to such factors, however, the new evidence cannot be regarded as anything other than a crushing blow to the high hopes raised by the publication of the provisional ratios based on the 1951 Census, and an extraordinary contrast to the apparent increasing success in reducing the social class gradient in *infant* mortality.

The persistence of very large local and regional variations in the incidence of particular diseases and of death from them (after standardising for age) also gives cause for concern, and any attempt at explanation is usually a highly complex and often baffling exercise. The material presented in map form in G. M. Howe's *National Atlas of Disease Mortality in the United Kingdom* cries out first for careful study of possible reasons and then for action aimed at reducing such discrepancies to a minimum.

Immigration and emigration

1964 (as noted at the top of p. 31) was the first year after 1957 to show a return to *outward* balances in migration to and from the United Kingdom. The size of these outward balances has varied, but we have continued to experience a net loss on migration account in each of the seven years 1964–70. The latest figures based on the International Passenger Survey, for 1970, do not show a very great change from the 1965 situation described on pp. 32 and 33. The Registrar General has since then revised his 1965 figures to show only 284,000 instead of 294,000 emigrants, and 206,000 instead of 219,000 immigrants, making the overall outward balance for that year 78,000 instead of 75,000. The corresponding figures for 1970 show 291,000 emigrants and 226,000 immigrants, giving an outward balance of 65,000 (the outward balances for 1966, 1967, 1968 and 1969 having been 83,000, 84,000, 56,000 and 87,000 respectively). In terms of citizenship, the outward balance of 65,000 for 1970 just quoted, resulted from an outward balance of 119,400 British (U.K.) citizens, and inward balances of 26,700 Overseas Commonwealth citizens and 27,600 'aliens'. In terms of broad occupational categories, the net overall loss of those who classified themselves as 'administrators, managers, and persons with professional and technological qualifications' was about 10,000 in 1970.

At the time this book was first published, discussion of the implications of these immigration and emigration data tended to focus on two issues, the so-called 'brain drain', and immigration from the new Commonwealth countries. Looking at the first of these issues, the report of the committee under the chairmanship of Dr F. E. Jones, mentioned as forthcoming on p. 34, duly appeared. A large number of recommendations was made with a view to attempting to check what the committee regarded as a major loss of engineers and technologists, and a slightly less serious loss of scientists, mainly between the ages of 25 and 35, at the height of their mental and physical powers and at the start of their most productive years. The theme was also taken up at the 1968 British Association meeting in Dundee. The only consoling, if partly fortuitous, aspect of the situation was felt to arise from the coming into force in July 1968 of the Unites States Immigration Act of 1965. This had the effect of abolishing the previous system of national quotas (favouring the skilled immigrant from Western Europe). As a result, would-be immigrants not already in the queue might have to wait as long as two years for a visa, and some forecasts suggested that the inflow of professional people from countries such as Britain might for some time be reduced to as little as a tenth of its previous size.

Less and less credence eventually came to be given both to the view that as a nation we were suffering from a shortage of scientists, and to the belief that such a shortage was being accentuated by a 'brain drain'. One reason was the publication in 1971 of *Persons with Qualifications in Engineering, Technology and Science 1959 to 1968* (Studies in Technological Manpower, No. 3), based on new data from the 1966 Census and elsewhere. It appeared that, in the 1960s, we had on balance been gaining rather than losing scientists; those returning from overseas, together with immigrants from other countries, more than made up for the emigrants. There did seem to be a net loss of engineers, but the numbers showed substantial year-to-year fluctuations. It was still a matter of concern that our National Health Service would clearly break down but for the services of medically-qualified people from overseas. One disturbing aspect of this was that the countries of origin of most of these immigrant doctors were desperately short of people with their skills.

The question in the 1966 Census which made available new data on numbers of scientists and technologists was, of course, couched in a form making it possible to obtain a picture of a much wider range of qualified personnel than this. Those coming into the 10 per cent sample were asked about qualifications obtained since the age of 18, and the nature and distribution of the stock of men and women with qualifications of all main types was shown in *Qualified Manpower in Great Britain* (1971). The 'flow' aspect was partly covered by annual official statistics of entry to and completion of courses of study in higher education. And since 1963 another official publication, *First Employment of University Graduates,* had shown what jobs or types of postgraduate training were taken up by graduates, in the year in which they completed their first degrees. Late in 1970 the first results of an *unofficial* six-year follow-up of a national sample of some 10,000 men and women who graduated in 1960 were published in *Six Years After* (Kelsall, Poole and Kuhn, Sheffield University), and it was possible for the first time to see the flows and counterflows into and out of different types of employment (gainful and otherwise), as well as many other aspects of the patterns of life of this important group of people.

When this book first appeared, the question of Commonwealth immigrants was very much a live issue and it has remained so ever since. In a broad sense Government policy has continued to be as described on p. 67, and its implementation has led to a continuing decline in the number of work-voucher immigrants from the 5,461 already quoted on p. 68 for 1966 to 4,978 in 1967; 4,691 in 1968; 4,021 in 1969; and 4,098 in 1970. It is worth noting that this relatively small figure includes significant numbers of holders of Category B vouchers, for applicants possessing certain special qualifications or skills—some 700 doctors, dentists and nurses, 250 teachers, 300 science and technology graduates, and 300 members of other professions.

Dependants accompanying, or coming to join, heads of households, around 42,000 in 1966, rose to nearly 53,000 in 1967, but have fallen to about 44,000, 34,000 and 27,000 in subsequent years. In addition, there were, in 1970, some 5,000 coming for settlement who had not been included under other headings (including about 1,600 holders of vouchers from the special allocation for U.K. passport holders, explained below). This makes in total a 1970 entry of rather less than 37,000 apparently intending to stay here more or less permanently, of whom nearly 7,000 were U.K. passport holders from East Africa, who form what is virtually a group of refugees, for helping whom Britain has a moral if not also a legal responsibility.

Part of the reduction in dependants admitted in 1968 and subsequently has arisen from a second Commonwealth Immigrants Act coming into force in March 1968; dependent children were no longer to be able to join a *single* parent in the United Kingdom without special permission, and no dependent father was to be admitted unless he was over 65. As part of a general 'tightening up' to meet criticisms that illegal and doubtfully legal entry was too easy, the period of time during which someone found to have entered illegally could be told to leave was extended from 24 hours after arrival to 28 days. At the same time provision was made for the relatively new case of Kenyan Asians with British citizenship; they were to be kept within a special annual quota of 1,500 work vouchers for British passport holders generally.

The two remaining related legislative changes of recent years may be very briefly mentioned. The Race Relations Act 1968 provided for the first time a legal framework within which various forms of discrimination and the exercise of racial prejudice could be discouraged, but its bearing on the problems with which we are concerned was indirect rather than direct. Similarly, the Immigration Act 1971 brought together many previously existing governmental powers with some additions, mainly of a permissive character, covering such matters as entry, residence, deportation, repatriation and the acquiring of citizenship. It did not of itself alter our policy on immigration, which was unkindly summed up by a writer in *New Society* (21 October 1971) as selfishly 'robbing the developing countries of their much needed doctors and dentists, and letting in only enough foreign labour to keep the tourist industry booming.'

There continued to be some doubt as to the present and probable future size of the addition to our population resulting from Commonwealth immigration. One of the first sources of official information on this since the peak years of inflow in the early 1960s was the Commonwealth Immigrant Tables of the 1966 Sample Census, which showed that some 853,000 people living in Great Britain had been born in the new Commonwealth, compared with 125,000 who had been born in the old Commonwealth of Australia, New Zealand and Canada. Taking account of the children born to immigrants after arrival here, and making a variety of rather complex assumptions about colour in relation to area of overseas origin, it appeared that what might be very loosely called the coloured immigrant population of Britain at that date was probably about 1,200,000.

The publication in July 1969 of *Colour and Citizenship* by E. J. B. Rose and others, making recommendations and reporting on a searching investigation under the auspices of the Institute of Race Relations, was an event of major importance. This study was, of course, principally concerned with much wider aspects than merely estimating probable future numbers of citizens whose pigmentation would differentiate them from the indigenous population. It did, however, include some estimates of this kind, taking official data as base, and assuming *inter alia* certain rates of inflow of dependants and a continued issue of work vouchers at about the current rate. Alternative fertility assumptions were then made. On the higher of these, a total coloured population of some 2,373,000 in Britain in 1986 might be expected; on the lower and more likely assumption the figure would be around 2,074,000.

All this did not satisfy critics such as Enoch Powell, who in February 1971 again characterised both official and unofficial estimates as gravely misleading. In his view, the available evidence suggested that the figure was already about two million and was likely, on present trends, to reach four million by the mid-1980s. This in its turn led the Runnymede Trust in the following month to produce some new unofficial but carefully constructed estimates. Starting from a 1969 baseline of, at the outside, 1,500,000, they came to the conclusion that even on the most generous assumptions of coloured population growth the 1985 figure could hardly be expected to exceed three million, and might well be as low as 2,250,000. So far as the *present* position is concerned, more up-to-date and reliable official data will be available when the relevant figures resulting from the 1971 Census are published.

The confusion was not made less by differences of view as to how one should define the people to be included in such calculations. In the educational sphere, for example, the current official form which schools have to fill in defines immigrants as children born outside the United Kingdom, *or* those born within the U.K. to parents who have arrived here since 1960. On this basis, some 3·5 per cent of pupils in England and Wales are classified as immigrants. Using other criteria you could, of course, arrive at a proportion considerably higher than this. Moreover, the continued application of the 'ten-year rule' is bound to mean that the official figures will increasingly be challenged as being out of date. So in 1971–72 the Select Committee on Race Relations and Immigration heard the views of interested parties on various possible revisions of the definition and it emerged, predictably, that almost any change could be objected to as being racist, or as so widening the field covered as to be absurd. Faced with this kind of dilemma it was not surprising that some critics felt the whole business of collecting and publishing figures of this type to be a pointless exercise. What mattered, they said, was to identify those children experiencing, or likely to experience, special educational and linguistic difficulties, and neither colour nor parental origin of themselves enabled you to do this.

Population projections

The projection discussed in the first edition was based on the estimated mid-1965 population, and was made at a time when for nearly a decade each successive annual total of live births had exceeded the preceding one. In these circumstances it was natural that, once the upward trend in births was seen to be more than a merely temporary phenomenon, the successive annual official projections should reflect this tendency, and show steadily larger populations than the preceding ones. It was equally obvious that, if the downturn in recorded births which began in 1965 showed signs of continuing for some time, the official projections would also have to be adjusted downwards. In the event, at least seven years of declining births have, as we saw, been recorded since then. It is therefore not surprising that the projection of the mid-1970 population gives a total for England and Wales in 2001 some 7,834,000 smaller than when the mid-1965 population formed the basis. Part of this difference relates, of course, to what has already happened even in the period of five years between the making of the two projections. Thus it is now clear that the number of births between mid-1965 and 1970 was considerably overestimated, and at the end of that period births were in fact taking place at a rate of at least 150,000 *less* annually than the numbers postulated.

The assumption regarding future births on which the official projection of the mid-1970 England and Wales population is based supposes a gradual increase to 862,000 in 1976; 884,000 in 1981; 974,000 in 1991; and 1,014,000 in 2001. The assumptions regarding future mortality trends, however, are not very different from those used on the earlier occasion. At ages under 40 for males and under 50 for females, death rates are assumed to decline until, by the year 2011 (further ahead, of course, than the 2001 end-date previously used) they are one half or less of present rates. Above these ages, the assumed rates of mortality reduction become progressively smaller, and they disappear altogether at ages beyond 90.

It was explained on p. 70 that the official projection of the mid-1965 England and Wales population assumed a modest net *inward* movement from all sources of some 53,000 dwindling to 18,000 in 1978–79 and subsequently. Developments of the last five years or so have made it necessary to assume instead an even smaller net inward movement, starting at only 5,000 and dwindling to zero in 1972–73, followed by a small net *outward* movement reaching 4,000 a year in 1976–77 and 10,000 a year in mid-1981 and beyond. As before, of course, it has to be remembered that these figures include assumed internal migration within the United Kingdom as well as overseas migration.

As can be seen, therefore, the main reason why the official projection for 2001 is now 58,589,000 instead of 66,423,000 is because of changed assumptions regarding future births. Are the current assumptions on this matter likely to prove more reliable than those of, say, five years ago? Part of the answer lies in the fact of an increasing realisation that figures of births that have already taken place, even in the recent past, are not of themselves a sufficient guide to the future. They need to be supplemented by special surveys to try and discover whether the intentions of women in such matters as size of family and spacing of births are changing. There had already been American family intentions enquiries in 1955 and 1960, and a continuous one beginning in 1962. And in this country doubts about the significance of the reversal of the upward movement of births in 1965 led the Registrar General in 1966 to ask for such an investigation to be carried out by the Social Survey, using an England and Wales sample of 6,300 women under 45 years old and married only once. This was done in 1967, and the results have been used in projections made since 1969. The report, Myra Woolf's *Family Intentions,* only became available to the general public in 1971.

It showed that women married after 1959 expected on an average to have slightly smaller families than their immediate predecessors; and that the differential was most marked in those social strata where the modal size of family was largest. An increasing use of more reliable methods of contraception was apparent.

The value of such surveys to those making projections depends very much on two factors—the speed with which they can receive the results, and the narrowness of the gap between intentions and achievement. On the first of these points, even a two-year delay between the questioning of the sample and the making available of the results may be too long, as the usefulness of the material is mainly short-term. On the second point John Peel, who conducted an enquiry of this kind in Hull five years ago and has kept in touch with the women in his sample since then, has found that nine out of ten seem to have achieved their stated goals. So the current official assumption that completed family size, for those marrying at ages under 45, will tend to average 2·5 or a little less, might be expected to have rather more validity, at least in the short-term, than the assumptions made before any family intentions studies had taken place in England.

Apart from the considerably smaller *size* of the projected England and Wales population in 2001 in the most recent estimate by comparison with that made five years earlier, other differences are comparatively minor. The 15–64 age group is expected to form 63 rather than 60 per cent of the total population, but this is roughly what it forms already of the estimated mid-1970 population. So the 'burden of dependency' in purely demographic terms is likely to be much what it is now. Children under 15 are, on current expectations, likely to form 24 rather than 28 per cent of the total (and to be some 4 million fewer than was previously expected). Those aged 65 and over form 12 instead of 11 per cent of the new projected population (and are some 300,000 fewer than in the old projection). The expected age structure is, in short, very similar to the one we have now, in mid-1970.

Another aspect of the expected future position to which some attention has recently been drawn arises from the matter of regional distribution. The anticipated growth rate of our population may or may not be acceptable nationally, but is it acceptable regionally? It is estimated that, in Great Britain as a whole, the proportion of land in urban use has risen, since the beginning of the present century, from about 4 per cent of the total land area to 8 per cent; and it might rise to 11 per cent by the end of the century. This may not sound very startling, but given that the regional distribution of the population only changes relatively slowly, is it not going to mean very severe land availability problems for, say, North-West England, the region with the highest average population density? Matters of this kind are discussed in the recent report (after five years study) of an inter-departmental group under the joint auspices of the Department of the Environment, the Scottish Office and the Welsh Office, *Long-Term Population Distribution in Great Britain*.

So far we have mainly been concerned with the size and distribution of the projected population. Has there been any significant change in attitudes regarding the *desirability* of the rate of future growth implied? A major new dimension was added to the debate on Britain's population needs by the publication in January 1972 of a manifesto, 'Blueprint for Survival' in the *Ecologist*, drawn up by the editor and his deputy, Edward Goldsmith and Robert Allen, and signed by thirty-three distinguished scientists, mainly botanists and zoologists. Very briefly, the argument was that chemical poisoning, pollution, and the side-effects of technological advance were leading towards an imminent breakdown of the natural life-support systems of the earth. Matters would be made worse by impending irremediable shortages of food, water and raw materials for other reasons as well. The only practicable answer for Britain, it was said, was to reverse present policies aimed at economic growth and plan for stabilisation or even reduction both of economic and population growth. And though the issue was a world one, Britain should curb her population expansion and try if possible to bring about a reduction of numbers from some 55 million to around 30 million. Substantial support for these proposals was forthcoming amongst medical men, and an active campaign to bring pressure on the Government rapidly gained momentum. Earlier, in May 1971, the Select Committee on Science and Technology, after reporting that Government action was urgently needed 'to prevent the consequences of population growth becoming intolerable for the everyday conditions of life' had recommended the setting up of a special office directly responsible to the Prime Minister to undertake and co-ordinate research and to publicise the consequences of excessive population expansion in the United Kingdom and the desirability of family planning. In a subsequent White Paper the view was expressed that the addition of a new piece of permanent official machinery would not at this stage be helpful; but it was promised that a team of specialists would be asked to carry out careful and dispassionate analyses in depth to provide the research basis for future population policy.

Many commentators felt that both the British ecologists and their medical supporters were, in the context of a country with one of the slowest population growth rates in the world, being quite unnecessarily alarmist. And it was certainly odd that the anti-natalist campaign in Britain should have been initiated at a time when, as we have seen, each official projection showed total numbers very much less than its predecessors. By no stretch of imagination could what was happening or expected to happen here be categorised as a population explosion, yet letters both in *The Lancet* and the *British Medical Journal* demanded urgent governmental and medical action to curb this. Groups already pressing for contraceptives and voluntary sterilisation to be made available free under the National Health Service have become more active recently. The current position is that most of the family planning clinics are provided by voluntary bodies; and that about a third of the local authorities give free advice to the public and, at the time of writing, only eleven provide free contraceptives as well. The largest of the voluntary bodies, the Family Planning Association has, however, in 1972 been given a £50,000 government grant for two experimental projects (at Runcorn, Cheshire and Coalville, Leicestershire) to discover the effects of and the problems arising in providing a complete and entirely free family planning service for everyone. The results of these projects seem likely to have a considerable bearing on future official policy in this matter. We should know for the first time, for example, what saving in public expenditure in supporting young children is apparently attributable to the provision of such a comprehensive service.

There is, however, as yet no sign that a zero, let alone a negative population growth rate for Britain commands wide support as an objective of policy either amongst demographers or the leaders of the main political parties. On the other hand, the economic and social implications of a declining population would almost certainly be drastically reassessed today by comparison with how they were viewed at the time of the Royal Commission. The conservationists, of course, argue that continuous population growth at a significant rate can in any case only, in Britain's circumstances, be a temporary phase, and that the sole question is *when* growth ceases, the only choice being whether (individually or collectively) we have willed the cessation or whether it has been forced on us by shortages and constraints of many types.

Sample Census 1966

It was explained on p. 7 that a population census took place midway between those of 1961 and 1971, questioning a 10 per cent sample of heads of households instead of the whole universe of such heads. No results were yet available when this book was first written; but since then there has been a steady stream of volumes of Tables to complete the planned total. The Commonwealth Immigrants Tables and those relating to qualified manpower have already been mentioned. Another set of Tables of particular interest (contained in three volumes for England and Wales and two for Scotland) showed not merely changes of residence in the year before census day (as the 1961 Census had previously done) but also in the *five* years preceding that day. Considerable interest has also been aroused by the availability for the first time of Tables relating to car ownership and where cars were kept; about 1,044,000 of the households in Great Britain, or 6 per cent of the total, were found to have two or more cars, and a further 38 per cent had one car.

Census 1971

One of the novel features of the 1971 Census lay in returning to the practice of a full count for all parts of the enquiry, as against the overall sampling in 1966 and the partial sampling in 1961. This had, of course, the advantage of greater accuracy and reliability, particularly in the figures for small areas; to offset this, the heads of more households were put to the trouble of furnishing some types of information, and the cost of the operation was greater.

So far as the questions asked were concerned, perhaps one of the main surprises was the dropping of many of those that there had, at earlier stages of discussion, been strong pressure to include. Some other countries ask at population census time about one's income, and it had certainly originally been planned to ascertain, on this occasion, the annual earnings of all those over 15 years of age to the nearest £100. In the event, a *voluntary* survey of incomes of all over that age in a 1 per cent sample of households took place in March 1972. So, too, had it been hoped to supplement knowledge of whither one journeyed to work and by what means of transport (the latter asked for the first time in 1966), by finding out how much time was taken up by such travel; but this also was reluctantly abandoned. Pressure from various quarters to find out about second home ownership, central heating and telephones was also, in the end, ineffective.

Not all intended new questions were dropped, however, and one of those retained and causing a great deal of ill-feeling related to parental areas of origin. There was, of course, nothing novel in asking about a person's country of birth at a population census in Britain, though on this occasion the year of first entering the United Kingdom had also to be given for all those born overseas. In the years immediately preceding the 1971 Census, however, local registrars were for the first time required to ask and record additional birthplace facts when registering 'flow' data. At registration of a birth or stillbirth the birthplace of *both* parents was to be noted; and at death registration, the birthplace of the deceased. So when, at the 1971 Census, questions were asked, for all those in the household, not only about country of birth but also about birthplaces of *both* parents, it was natural that those concerned to preserve the traditional rights of immigrants and of ethnic minorities should have looked on this development in official data collection with extreme suspicion. The official justification advanced was that only in this way could special needs be identified and the success or failure of policies designed to meet these needs be properly assessed. The counter argument was that the collection and presentation of data distinguishing between areas of origin, far from being a neutral activity, was in itself discriminatory, and implied that one's ethnic background was important.

Two closely related issues came to a head incidental to the 1971 Census—that of confidentiality, and that of the legitimacy of asking for certain kinds of information. On the first, although safeguards as stringent as those applying on previous occasions were again in force, not everyone was satisfied that they were stringent enough, and there was the associated criticism of the selling of data (even though in a form where no individual could be identified) to commercial undertakings. On the second issue, refusal to answer some or all of the questions (and prosecution in consequence) was certainly on a larger scale than previously; and when the leader of the Liberal Party at one stage announced his intention of not filling in parts of the form, a particularly low point in public acceptability of what was being asked for seemed to have been reached. Though another is scheduled for 1976, some commentators who themselves saw no objection to the census either on grounds of confidentiality or the nature of some of the questions asked, nevertheless speculated as to whether the 1971 Census might prove to be the last national count of this kind. For once individualised data collection (on the lines described on pp. 11–13) has become firmly established, such periodic counts may no longer be as necessary. The potential dangers in storing personal data capable of being used to one's disadvantage would, however, be increased rather than diminished by a development of this type, and the recent introduction of a Bill to curb possible misuse of data banks is symptomatic of considerable, if sometimes ill-founded, public unease on this matter.

Index

(Note : material in Appendix 2 is not included in the Index)

Abel-Smith, B., 93, 102
Aberdeen, 49
'activity rate', 8–10, 81–2
address, change of usual, 41–6
age-structure, 2, 8–10, 27–8, 33, 59–63, 73–4, 80–3, 88
Allcorn, D. H., 52–3
Arie, T., 98
Australia, 26, 32–3, 34

Banks, J. A., 98
Banks, O., 98
Banton, M. P., 100
Bedford, 37
Beveridge, Lord, 61
Birmingham, 37, 77
birth rate, *see* fertility
birthplace, 11, 35–7, 95
births, illegitimate, 22
Blomfield, J. M., 98
Bonham, D. G., 98
'boom in babies', 21–3, 70, 94
Booth, C., 19
Boreham, J., 101
Bowen, I., 97
Bradford, 37
Bradlaugh-Besant trials, 18
'brain drain', 33–5, 64–6
Bristol, 37, 39
British Aerospace Companies, Society of, 34

British Isles, 14–17, 25, 35, 71, 79
'bulge in births', 20, 23, 70, 74, 82
'burden of dependency', 61, 74
Butler, N. R., 98

Canada, 32–3, 34
Cannan, E., 89
Caribbean, 36
Carr-Saunders, A. M., 97
Carrier, N. H., 99
Carter, A., 101
Census 1801, 15–16
    1821, 16–17
    1871, 16, 29
    1881, 15–16
    1891, 5, 16
    1901, 14–17
    1911, 16, 47, 64
    1921, 16–17, 28, 51
    1931, 16, 28, 29, 35, 51–2, 60, 72–4
    1951, 5–7, 16, 28, 39–40, 47, 51–2
    1961, 5–11, 14–17, 35–6, 41–6, 53, 56–7, 61, 64, 93, 95–7
    1966, 7, 93
Ceylon, 26, 33
Channel Islands, 14
classification changes, 6–7

Cole, D., 100
Committee on Economic and
    Financial Problems of Pro-
    vision for Old Age, 62, 100
Commonwealth, 6, 22, 29–37, 66–8,
    71–2, 92–3, 95, 99
Commonwealth Immigrants Act
    1962, 23, 30, 33, 36, 67–8, 97
Conurbation:
    Central Clydeside, 38
    Greater London, 35–6, 38,
        39, 42–3
    Merseyside, 35, 38, 42–3
    South-East Lancashire, 35,
        38, 42–3
    Tyneside, 35, 38, 42–5
    West Midlands, 35, 38, 42–3, 46
    West Yorkshire, 35, 38, 42–3
conurbations, 6, 35–6, 38–9, 95
Coventry, 37
Cox, P. R., 97
'cultural lag', 48–9
Cyprus, 36

data, individualised, 11–13
data, types of population, 5–13
Davison, R. B., 100
death rate, see mortality
Debate, House of Commons,
    13/2/67, 34
    House of Commons, 17/2/67,
        92–3
    House of Lords, 3/11/66, 67–8
Denmark, 25–6
density, varying, 39–41
Dick, A., 101
'disappearing spinster', 59
Douglas, J. W. B., 48, 98
'drift from countryside', 38–41

'drift to the South', 40–1, 46
    71, 76–9
Dudley, 37

Edinburgh, 39
Eire, 14, 25, 30–1
emigration, see migration
England and Wales, 1, 5, 8, 14–17,
    24–8, 29–31, 35–46, 47–8,
    49–51, 59–64, 69–79, 93,
    95–101
Eversley, D. E. C., 101
expectation of life, 2, 18, 25–7,
    50–3, 58–63

Family Census 1946, 6, 53–6, 96
family limitation/planning, 18–23,
    26, 53–7, 58–9, 64, 70, 84–5,
    87–94, 96, 98–9, 101
fertility, 2, 15, 18–23, 53–7, 58–9,
    70, 80, 87–9, 95–101
Finlayson, A., 99
forecasts, general manpower, 80–3,
    96–7, 101
    national population, 69–75,
        100–1
    regional population, 75–9, 92–3,
        100–1
    skilled manpower, 83–6, 96–7,
        101
France, 19, 25–6
Friedlander, D., 99

Gallup Poll, 92
Gavron, H., 99
General Register Office, see
    Registrar General
Glass, D. V., 53–4, 96, 98, 102
Glass, R., 66–7, 100

Government Actuary, 69
Great Britain, 8–11, 14–17, 36–7, 38–9, 48–9, 53–7, 64, 66, 69, 87–9, 91, 93, 95–101
'Great Depression', 18
Grebenik, E., 53–4, 96

H.M. Forces, 1
Hawkes, N., 100
High Wycombe, 37
Hogg, Q., 65
Houghton, D., 92–3
'household', definition of, 36
housing, 63–4, 91, 96–7
Huddersfield, 37

Illsley, R., 49, 52–3, 98, 99
immigration, *see* migration
India, 26, 33, 36–7
individualised data, 11–13
infant mortality, 24–5, 47–50, 98
intelligence, decline in national level of, 89–91
International Passenger Survey, 31–3, 35
Ireland, 35, 78–9, 87
Isaac, J., 99
Isle of Man, 14
Italy, 25

Jamaica, 36
Jeffery, J. R., 99
Jones, D. C., 97
Jones, F. E., 34

Kelsall, R. K., 55, 84–5, 101
Kiser, C. V., 98
Klein, V., 99

labour, changing demand for, 82
Leeds, 37
Leicester, 37
Lewis-Faning, E., 96
Lipworth, L., 49, 98
Liverpool, 37
living conditions, crowded, 36, 48, 63–4
London, 36, 39–40, 77, 79, 95
London School of Economics, 88

McCleary, G. F., 102
McKeown, T., 98
Malta, 36
Malthus, T. R., 87–9
Manchester, 37
Manchester Guardian, 51
manpower, general, *see* forecasts
manpower, qaulified, 7–11, 34, 65–6, 96–7
marriage, 20–3, 28, 53–7, 58–9, 81–6, 87–8, 95–9
Marsh, D. C., 97
Matras, J., 98
Mauritius, 88–9
Medawar, P. B., 98
medical practioners, 33–4, 65
middle-aged married woman, role of the, 58–9
migration, internal, 15, 38–46, 76–9, 92–4, 96, 99
migration overseas, 6, 15, 22–3, 28, 29–37, 64–8, 70–2, 76–9, 80, 82, 87, 92–3, 95–100
Minister for Science, 7
Ministry of Technology, 34
Ministry of Labour, 7–8, 68, 97, 100
misunderstanding, sources of, 1–4

Monmouthshire, 5, 14–15
Moore, R., 100
mortality, 2, 3, 15, 17, 18, 24–8, 47–53, 58–9, 69–70, 80, 88–9, 95–101
Moser, C. A., 97, 99
Myrdal, A., 99

natality, *see* fertility
National Advisory Council on the Training and Supply of Teachers, 85, 101
National Birthday Trust, 49, 98
National Health Service, 51, 92–3
National Insurance Act 1911, 19
National Plan 1965, 76
nationality, 11, 95
'nature-nurture', controversy, 90
natural increase, 29–30, 72, 74–5, 87–9
Netherlands, 25–6
Newcastle upon Tyne, 37, 99
New Towns, 40–1
New Zealand, 26, 32–3
Northern Ireland, 14–17, 25–6, 29–31, 69, 71, 78–9, 93, 95
Norway, 25–6
Notting Hill, 66
Nottingham, 37, 66

occupational distribution, 6–7, 9–10, 33
O'Connor, M., 100
old age, 59–63, 81–2, 100
Oversea Migration Board, 67, 96
'overspill', 40, 76–7, 79

Pakistan, 30, 33 36–7
Pierce, R. M., 98

'population at risk', 1–3, 47, 49
Population Investigation Committee, 98
population, 'optimum', 89
population policy, 91–4
theories, 87–91
'population', varying meanings explained, 1
poverty, 19, 48–50, 92–3
projections, *see* forecasts
race relations, 66–8, 99–100
Record, R. G., 98
Reddaway, W. B., 101
Regional Economic Planning Councils, 41, 77, 100–1
Registrar General, 15–16, 21–2, 34, 36, 41–4, 47–53, 56, 60, 69, 78, 95–101
registration data, 11
reproduction rates, 74–5
retirement, 61–2
Rex, J., 100
Richmond, A. H., 100
Roberts, B. C., 101
Roshier, R. J., 99
Rowntree, G., 98
Rowntree, J. A., 99
Royal Commission on the Distribution of the Industrial Population, 40, 96, 99
Royal Commission on Population, 19–21, 53–5, 96

sample, 10 per cent, 4, 6–8, 41–3, 93
sampling, 3–4, 31–2
school-leaving age, 80–3
scientific and technological qualifications, possession of, 7–11, 95–6, 101

Scotland, 8, 14–17, 25–6, 29–31, 35, 38, 40, 49, 69, 71–2, 78–9, 90, 93, 95
Scott, W., 55, 99
 exes, ratio between the, 2, 8–10, 25–8, 33, 64, 70, 73–4, 80–3, 88
Sheffield, 37, 39, 64, 77, 79
Shenfield, B. E., 100
Slough, 37
Smethwick, 37
Smith, J. H., 101
social class gradient, 47–50, 90, 98
Social Survey (Central Office of Information), 31–2
South Africa, 32–3, 34, 36
Spicer, C. C., 49, 98
Standard Regions, old style, 102–3
    East and West Ridings, 42–3, 45–6
    Eastern, 42–3, 45–6
    London and South Eastern, 42–3, 45–6
    Midland, 42–3, 45–6
    North Midland, 42–3, 45–6
    North Western, 42–3, 45–6
    Northern, 42–6
    South Western, 42–3, 45–6
    Southern, 42–3, 45–6
    Wales, 42–3, 45–6
Standard Regions, revised, 103–4
    East Anglia, 44, 77–9
    East Midland, 44, 77–9
    North, 44, 77–9
    North West, 44, 77–9
    South East, 44, 77–9
    South West, 44, 77–9
    Wales, 44, 77–9
    West Midland, 44, 77–9

Yorkshire and Humberside, 44, 77–9, 101
Stonham, Lord, 67–8
'surplus of women', 28, 59, 73
Sweden, 25–6

teachers, 2–3, 10, 55–6, 59, 83–6
Thompson, B., 99
Titmuss, R. M., 102
Townsend, P., 62–3, 93, 102

United Kingdom, 14–15, 29–33, 67–8, 69, 71–2, 80–3, 93, 100
United Nations, 97, 100
United States, 25–6, 29, 32–3, 34
'unproductive clerk', 55, 90
'urban dispersal', 39–41, 76–7
Utting, J. E. G., 100

'V-effect', 55

'wastage', 84–6
Wales, 5, 14–17, 40–6, 97
Watford, 41
Wedderburn, D., 100
'W-effect', 51–2
West Bromwich, 37
West Indies, 22, 30, 33, 36–7, 66–7, 99
Wolstenholme, G. E. W., 100
Wolverhampton, 37
working population, see forecasts, general manpower
World War I, 17, 18, 20, 28
World War II, 20, 24, 29–30, 39
Wrong, D. H., 97

York, 79